THE SAI WAY

THE SAI WAY

Shirdi ke Sai Baba in a never-before perspective

Suresh Haware

BLOOMSBURY
NEW DELHI • LONDON • OXFORD • NEW YORK • SYDNEY

BLOOMSBURY INDIA
Bloomsbury Publishing India Pvt. Ltd
Second Floor, LSC Building No. 4, DDA Complex, Pocket C – 6 & 7,
Vasant Kunj, New Delhi 110070

BLOOMSBURY, BLOOMSBURY INDIA and the Diana logo
are trademarks of Bloomsbury Publishing Plc

First published in India 2021
This edition published 2021

ISBN: PB: 978-93-54350-86-3; e-Book: 978-93-54350-88-7
2 4 6 8 10 9 7 5 3 1

Typeset in Manipal Technologies Limited
Printed and bound in India

MIX
Paper from
responsible sources
FSC® C016779

To find out more about our authors and books, visit www.bloomsbury.com and sign up for our newsletters

I dedicate this book to the fond and
loving memories of Sadguru Shri Sai Baba,
experienced by myself and my wife Nalini,
especially of the last five years
that we shall cherish forever.

CONTENTS

FOREWORD

I am happy to see a new book on the teachings of Shri Sai Baba from Dr Suresh Haware, the Chairman of Shri Sai Baba Sansthan Trust, Shirdi, and a nuclear scientist. The Sai philosophy, spirituality and information are presented very well in the book.

Thousands of devotees from a number of countries visit Shirdi. I also visit Shirdi as a devotee of Sai Baba along with my family. Baba's teachings of shraddha and saburi and sab ka malik ek look simple, but it is very difficult to put them in practice. Instant gratification has become the wish of the day. People want things immediately, even though everything has its own gestation period. Everything happens in its own time, and it is good to wait for them to happen naturally. Unnecessary haste has disturbed the world. Saburi has very much become the need of the hour.

It is a unique fact about Sai Baba that His temples are spread all over the world. Sai Baba's temples are in all corners of India, with the maximum number of them in Andhra Pradesh and Telangana. There are Sai Baba temples in 43 countries in the world, including the USA, Canada, England, France, Germany, Australia, New Zealand, and the Sai Movement is one of the largest spiritual movements in the world. It is noteworthy that Dr Haware has attempted twice to integrate all these

Sai Baba trusts by organising the Global Sai Temple Summits.

Dr Haware is a nuclear scientist. I am familiar with his approach and way of working. He has brought a lot of transformation in the face and image of Shirdi.

It is pleasing to know about the five important social initiatives in Shirdi taken by Dr Suresh Haware and his team. All these are very innovative, and I find that the blood donation drive is one of the most important of these initiatives. It is true that there is no alternative to human blood. I was told that the blood so collected at Shirdi is forwarded through 25 blood banks in the villages and remote areas in Maharashtra. This will definitely help reduce blood shortage. Another wonderful initiative is that of making agarbatti (incense sticks) from the daily floral offerings on Sai Baba's samadhi. Many temples can take up this lesson from Shirdi. It has saved flowers from being thrown in the garbage; rather, it has respected the emotions of the devotees attached with these flowers. The most noteworthy thing is that it has provided jobs to 200 needy women and generated wealth.

The initiative of cleaning Shirdi is really worthy of appreciation. I think Shirdi has shown us the way that temples should take responsibility to make the areas clean and green. Shirdi became the third cleanest city in the country and has twice earned prize worth 15 crores. I was told that in the survey conducted by *India Today* of temple towns, Shirdi came out to be the cleanest and won the first prize, awarded in the august presence of Hon. Shri Ramnath Kovind, President of India. The Sai Baba Temple in Shirdi has devised a novel scheme of allowing devotees to offer their services. I was told that more than 25,000 devotees have already participated in this scheme and were blessed by Sai Baba.

This book by Dr Haware has touched upon some very important aspects of devotees' interest and provides important information about the temple. It also discusses the philosophy of Sai Baba in a very simple but concrete way. The photographs presented in this book will say a lot and add to the credentials of the book. I find that it is a must-read book on Sai Baba.

Sai is now a global deity, and therefore the book by Dr Haware will reach the devotees all over the world and will enrich them. I extend my best wishes to Dr Suresh Haware and all Sai devotees.

Om Sai Ram!

Dr Satheesh Reddy
Aerospace Scientist
Chairman, Defence Research and Development Organisation (DRDO)
and Secretary, Department of Defence R&D, Government of India

BLESSINGS

I had the pleasure of going through *The Sai Way*, authored by Dr Suresh Haware, Chairman, Shri Sai Baba Sansthan Trust, Shirdi (popularly known as the Sansthan). He was appointed Chairman on 28 July 2016 and still continues to hold the position. Haware is a nuclear scientist and worked at Bhabha Atomic Research Centre (BARC) for 27 years. Later, he became the chairman and managing director of Haware Properties, Navi Mumbai, Maharashtra. Thus, he had substantial experience of running a big business organisation before joining the Sansthan.

I have had direct contact with most of those who served as the chairman of the Sansthan since 1989, when I first visited Shirdi. Prominent personalities from various walks of life, such as politicians, retired IAS officers and doctors, had functioned as the Chairman of the Sansthan and had contributed a lot towards the management, smooth running and upgrading of the facilities needed in Shirdi during their tenure. Needless to say that over the last three decades or so, the number of visitors at Shirdi has grown exponentially. From an average of about 5,000, the number of devotees visiting each day had increased to around 50,000 before the onset of the COVID-19 pandemic, when it drastically reduced.

However, Dr Haware's appointment as Chairman in July 2016 may be considered as both different and significant. Shirdi Sai Baba's Mahasamadhi centenary year was celebrated from 1 October 2017 till 18 October 2018. Dr Haware, as the chairman of the Sansthan, was entrusted with the unique responsibility of conducting the year-long Mahasamadhi festivities, which included several major events and a plethora of minor events, virtually on a daily basis. During this period, the Hon'ble President of India, Hon'ble Prime Minister of India and a large number of important visitors from India and abroad visited the shrine of Baba and participated in various events. As many as 3.5 crore devotees visited Shirdi during this period. It could not have been an easy task for the Sansthan and Mr Haware to take care of the mammoth gatherings. The planning and arrangements for the event, catering to all the needs, including logistics, of the devotees visiting from all over the globe, administration and running of the numerous religious activities and coordination with different stakeholders involved in the celebrations must have given Dr Haware rich and unique experiences which no other chairman had received in the past.

Therefore, this book, titled *The Sai Way*, contains the vast experience of Dr Haware and is going to be a great guide not only to the Sansthan but also for research scholars and readers in the future. New experience and practices will surely help other temples in running and updating their affairs. Many of the infrastructural and other activities introduced during the centenary year can be taken as models in future—pertaining to the construction of roads, buildings, water, electricity, sewerage systems, civic care, medical care, creation of adequate board and lodging spaces, proper management of transportation, maintenance of law and order, control of crime and many more. This would have called for vast networking with other stakeholders like the Sai Baba temples and organisations all over the world, between the Sansthan, the Government of Maharashtra, civic bodies and various types of service-providing organisations. It must have been a Herculean task that called for wholehearted commitment and a mission mode of functioning combined with faith in Shirdi Sai Baba.

The approach of writing this book is clearly stated by the author in the prologue. Further, the essence of his experience in dealing with Shirdi-related affairs as the Chairman of the Sansthan and his personal experiences as a devotee of Shirdi Sai Baba leads him to declare in unequivocal terms, 'I am writing this with full responsibility as a nuclear scientist that there is something beyond science.' It seems to be this belief that gave him the conviction and strength to perform to the best of his ability despite all the odds that he faced while handling this significant task. It is easy to have faith in science as science is based on empiricism. However, it is difficult to discover the science of faith. Spiritually evolved personalities such as Shri Shirdi Sai Baba experienced and propagated the science of faith.

I have observed that Dr Haware is a patient listener with a proactive approach to new ideas. After he took over as the chairman of the Sansthan, we met at a Shirdi Sai Baba temple located in Noida during his visit to Delhi.

What struck me about him was his sober and genuine approach to conducting the heavy responsibility of the Sansthan with the zeal of a missionary.

Most of the books on Baba written by Indian authors and a few writers from abroad are mostly from the angle of bhakti. Research studies on Baba are highly lacking. During the Global Sai Summit held at Shirdi on 11 and 12 December 2017, I had suggested that such research studies be undertaken in universities, particularly in Maharashtra. I had also suggested a new approach to the writing of a book on Baba. I must congratulate Dr Haware for coming up with a book with a different approach and narrative. The book, in short, narrates the endeavour of the author to convert the Sai faith to 'seva'. 'Seva' means rendering service in the best possible way for the cause of 'human beings'. This Baba practised in Shirdi till the day of His Mahasamadhi.

The two cardinal principles of Shri Sai, as also brought out by the author, are 'shraddha' (faith) in God and Sadguru with 'saburi' (patience under all conditions). After Sai Baba's Mahasamadhi, the Sansthan was formed to carry on the wishes of Sai Baba.

Dr Haware is a person with a high level of sensitivity towards the events and happenings at Shirdi as he faced them. Without such sensitivity, it is not possible to write what he has written in the 'Sai Bhakti' and 'Sai Anubhuti' sections of this book. Many devotees of Shri Sai Baba have experienced that, when carrying on with such onerous duties, one faces difficulties and has to handle them through a zigzag path; but in the end, the goal is achieved. As history indicates, during Baba's time, some of the ardent devotees who worked for the cause of Baba could not follow a linear path either. *Shri Sai Satcharita* is replete with such anecdotes.

Shirdi Sai Baba devotees mostly believe that whatever happens with respect to Sai Baba only happens because of His will. Here is the case of Dr Haware, who was jostled in Baba's samadhi temple in Shirdi and had decided never to revisit it. However, he was placed as the chairman of the Sansthan at Shirdi. Can we call it a miracle or 'leela' in the sense of the term as devotees generally believe? Perhaps Shirdi Sai Baba knows the best.

Of the many innovative programmes that the Sansthan has updated/introduced under the leadership of Dr Haware are to recycle the throwaway waste products like the flowers (offered to Shri Sai) into incense sticks, thereby generating employment for men and women and increasing the turnover of the Sansthan; a collaborative campaign between the Sansthan, the local municipal council and local residents to clean up the city using various types of technology, including the anaerobic bio-digestion process; procurement of 128 new machines including a cath lab, CT scan and MRI machines for the two hospitals serving under Sansthan i.e., Shri Sainath Hospital and Shri Sai Baba Hospital. It is a creditable venture to make Shri Sainath Hospital entirely free of cost from 1 January 2017.

Also, a number of blood donation camps have been organised. Devotees offer to donate blood with the same spirit as when offering flowers, fruits, etc. to God. It is a unique union of shraddha with service. It is a mammoth task to cook meals for 70,000 to one lakh people every day. The offering of prasad free of cost from 1 January 2017 was another major step, since almost 70,000 to one lakh meals were prepared per day. The Sai Sevak Scheme was initiated to encourage volunteers to complete their service in many ways.

I wish that Dr Haware writes more books on this subject as he has become a vast repository of knowledge as the chairman of the Sansthan for so long. *The Sai Way* is a great contribution to Sai literature, and I am sure, it will be appreciated by Sai devotees and general readers.

Dr C.B. Satpathy (I.P.S)
Director General Police (U.P.), Retd.
New Delhi

PROLOGUE

My becoming Chairman of the Shirdi Sai Baba Sansthan is a sheer coincidence. Some years back, my family and I visited Shirdi for darshan. The queue was orderly until we reached Baba's samadhi, but once we reached there, we got pushed out by the people crowding and shoving each other. We did not even get proper darshan. On coming out, I said to my wife, 'After this, I will never visit Shirdi again. This is my last visit to Shirdi.' I did not go to Shirdi after that.

One day I received a call from Hon. Devendra Fadnavis, the then CM of Maharashtra. He said, 'We are considering appointing you as the Chairman of Shirdi Sai Baba Sansthan.' I immediately recalled my experience and shared it with Devendra ji. He laughed and said, 'Perhaps Baba himself is calling you.' Taking this as a sign of Sai prasad, I decided to accept the responsibility of Shirdi.

The Western world has made much material progress. The lives of the people there have a wonderful dynamism, but they have relatively lesser mental peace. In comparison, the Eastern world is peaceful. They have a good degree of peace of mind but there is not much material progress or dynamism, barring a few countries. The question is how to combine these two tendencies and create a world where there is material progress and, at the same time, there is peace. How do we achieve the best combination of dynamism and peace? The answer lies in the Indian Vedanta philosophy. It is prevalent in the teachings of almost all the saints of India, including the Sai philosophy. It propagates the eternal principles of life and living that do not change with time.

The Sai philosophy of shraddha and saburi and sab ka mailk ek is very easy to understand but equally difficult to practise. And unless the philosophy is put into practice, it has no value. Only spiritual growth and spiritual practice can ensure a peaceful yet dynamic life.

There have been many books written about Sai. They lead one to ask, why one more? And why do I want to write it? The answer lies in my five years of Sai Anubhuti. Sai Anubhuti is not theoretical, it is practical. It cannot be expressed in words.

Sai ways are not linear, they are criss-cross. For the last five years, I have experienced a totally different world. I write this with full responsibility as a nuclear scientist and state that there is something beyond science. I have endeavoured to present Sai ways from a new and never-before perspective. I am sure that Sai devotees will love it.

Om Sai Ram!

INTRODUCTION

Sai philosophy has two aspects—Sai Leela and Sai Seva. People are well versed with Sai Leela. Sai Seva, on the other hand, is less known, but it is more pronounced in Sai's teachings. Sai Leela refers to the manifestations of His divine powers, such as the burning of oil lamps with water when a shopkeeper refused to give oil, His curing/healing patients and safeguarding the town from an epidemic. All these are considered His miracles. There may be some logic, reason or science behind each of His acts, but no one has tried to analyse them. Most devotees strongly believe in these mystic events, love them and admire them. Rarely are they open to scrutiny, whether scientific or otherwise. Devotees strongly believe that He possessed extraordinary power.

He used to ask for bhiksha (alms) at five houses in Shirdi every day, and that would be His staple for the day for Himself and the devotees. Begging for alms is not proper translation of bhiksha, as bhiksha involves giving up the ego and thus includes an element of devotion. It can be called devotional begging. He would grind the grains received as bhiksha and cook the food Himself. He would serve it to the devotees and only then would He consume it Himself. His motive was annadaan. He would pick up a broom and would

Himself clean the temple premises every day. His objective was to ensure cleanliness. He would plant trees and water them every day—the basic thought behind this act was environmental care. He would care for cows and animals, organise bhajan and kirtan—the objective was to encourage cultural activities. He would Himself wrestle and would organise wrestling matches every year at Shirdi. This was His way of promoting sports. He would nurse patients and take all the medical care to cure them. Healthcare was the motive behind this action. He would play with children and teach them good values to educate them. His every action was a service to society and humanity; we can call it Sai Seva. Here again I shall draw your attention to the meaning of seva. It is not mere service; rather it is service with devotion and love. I deeply feel that His Sai Leela manifestations were also partly for the purpose of seva. The book discusses all these aspects of Sai philosophy in detail.

Sai Bhakti, as taught by Sai Baba, is very simple to talk about but very difficult to practise. It is nothing but shraddha and saburi, both of which are necessary. Shraddha, a very important aspect of the human mindset, cannot be equated directly with faith, as that is a very small word to describe it. We can say shraddha is faith imbued with devotion and love. We observe that when a person needs healthcare, they consult only the doctor in whom they have trust, faith, shraddha, and this is not based only on the doctor's expertise. Similarly, when a person chooses a goldsmith or a grocer or an item of daily need, they go to only those places that inspire faith. Thus, faith is not just a word but a deep-rooted experience that helps us decide. Shraddha is the basic foundation for human beings. If the foundation is strong, you can build a tall building on it and not otherwise. Shraddha builds your confidence and is, therefore, a necessary facet of the human personality.

Saburi is not merely patience; it implies an element of devotion as well. Saburi then is patience imbued with devotion and love. The lack of saburi is the root of most human problems. If you listen to someone patiently, 90 per cent of their problems are resolved then and there. People need patient listening. Listening is an art, and it has to be developed properly. It is only with practice and time that you will master this art. I once went to the famous Siddhivinayak Temple at Prabhadevi, Mumbai. I found a solid silver mouse (mushaka) placed in the temple premises. Devotees were pouring their sorrows into the ears of this silver mouse. There was a queue before the mouse, and devotees waited to open up to the mouse with their story. They believe that the mouse is the messenger of Lord Ganesh and that their sorrows will directly reach the Lord through the mouse. This is somewhat similar to the confession service available in religious centres. In response to the popular demand by devotees, the temple management decided to place four such silver mice in the temple premises. All the mice are busy listening to the sorrows of the devotees. Irrespective of whether there is science behind this happening, it is clear that being heard is a necessity. This need arises from the increasing lack of saburi in society. About 99 per cent of people give up before they receive the fruit; only the one who is patient succeeds. Saburi does not come naturally—it has to be learnt. If you give it enough time, any wound is healed, any anger soothed, any enmity pacified, any fire extinguished, any ocean crossed and any mountain scaled. All you need is saburi.

'Sab ka mailk ek' is a universal teaching of Sai Baba. It is a universally accepted truth that God is one—people view God differently. All spiritual schools of thought express this idea. There are differences in the words of prayer, in the holy symbols and the rituals practised, but the underlying principle is the same, i.e. sab ka mailk ek. This age-old principle discovered by the sages through self-realisation has also been discussed in the book.

Somewhat misleadingly, superstitions about Sai Baba have spread. Some time ago, the news spread that an image of Sai Baba appeared on the wall of Dwarakamai in Shirdi Temple, where Baba used to stand. The security guard was the first to notice it. The news spread like wildfire and thousands of people gathered. The media would not miss such an occurrence, and reporters appeared to shoot the images and cover the story. Many people saw something on the wall that resembled Sai Baba. The next day, the TV news channels were discussing this incident. They approached me for my opinion. I have presented my views very logically and have discussed all aspects of this event later in this book.

Once I was invited as the chief guest for a national conference organised by Mumbai University's Department of Commerce. It was held in their Kalina campus and was attended by more than a thousand students and professors. When my turn came to speak and I approached the podium, I was greeted by the slogan 'Sainath Maharaj ki jai'. I started my talk by interacting with the students. I asked how many of the audience had been to Shirdi; around 90 per cent of the students raised their hands. Then I asked them whether they were aware that there is a solar-operated mega kitchen at Shirdi that works almost round the clock and feeds around one lakh devotees every day? Not a 1,000 or 10,000, but the huge number of one lakh. And this gigantic task is undertaken every day. Did they know that there are two hospitals at Shirdi with a total capacity of 575 beds? And that one of those is a super-specialty hospital? Did they know that the temple has accommodation for 20,000 devotees? Did they know that the temple manages schools and colleges with a total capacity of around 6,000 students? Did they know that the temple has more than 5,000 direct employees and an almost equal number of indirect ones? The reaction of the audience to all these questions was one of baffled surprise. The students were not aware of these things. Thereafter, I realised that even most of the devotees are not aware of this vast scope of activities and the work of the temple. Therefore, I have devoted some pages of this book to creating awareness among readers. It will provide authentic information about Shirdi, the holy place of pilgrimage for Sai devotees.

We have undertaken a number of social initiatives in Shirdi. These projects are innovative concepts, such as the daily blood donation drive. This is the most important initiative and is unique to Shirdi. We have involved 25 blood banks in this project. They ensure the daily collection of donated blood in the Sai Baba Temple premises at Shirdi. The blood donors are given a certificate and are allowed direct darshan of Baba. Initially, 15 to 20 devotees used to donate blood daily. As the concept/scheme spread, the number of donors went up to 150 to 200 devotees per day. The response was phenomenal. Annually more than 50,000 units of blood are now collected at Shirdi and supplied to hospitals all over Maharashtra. We defined the scheme thus: 'Tirupati mein keshdan, Shirdi mein raktadan' ('Hair donation at Tirupati, blood donation at Shirdi'). Other notable initiatives include the recycling of floral offerings on Sai Baba's samadhi for manufacturing agarbattis; the Clean Shirdi Movement, which won the first prize from Hon. President of India and the Sai Sevak Scheme, which allows devotees to serve at the temple for a week. These initiatives have touched the hearts of lakhs of devotees and have hence earned a place in this book.

A number of initiatives in infrastructure development have also been undertaken in Shirdi, such as the inauguration of the Sai Baba International Airport, the Modern Educational Complex, the Darshan Queue Complex, the Solid Waste Management Plant, the Solar Power Plant, the Sai Knowledge Park with a planetarium and wax museum. The response to the air service has been so enthusiastic that the Shirdi airport has now become the third busiest airport in Maharashtra after Mumbai and Pune. The book contains an account of these initiatives.

Very few devotees know how the idol of Sai Baba was carved out and how it arrived in Shirdi. This interesting history has been included in the book.

There are around 8,000 Sai Baba temples in India and around 450 Sai Baba temples in other countries. We undertook the task of identifying and uniting these temples under the banner of Global Sai Temples Summit; two such summits were organised at Shirdi in 2017 and 2018. This project was aimed at making Shirdi a place of sangam for all these Sai Baba temples. An account of this endeavour is also included in the book.

The book also discusses some controversies that have been associated with the birthplace of Sai Baba.

There are around 6.5 lakh (0.65 million) villages in India. We also possess 20 lakh (2 million) schools and colleges and around 30 lakh (3 million) major temples. It is interesting to note that the number of temples in our country surpasses the number of schools and colleges. It also gives us an idea about the scale of social influence that temples can exert.

In the olden days, the temple used to be the centre of the town. All the activities of the town would take place around the temple. Today, these temples in India, taken together, generate huge wealth. An observation of various temples reveals two common shortcomings. Naturally, there are exceptions, but these two shortcomings are generally apparent in most temples. The first is that these temples are unorganised, and the second is that they lack discipline. Therefore, I perceive a need for teaching temple management. It should be taught at universities, just like courses in marketing management and finance management. Formal training will generate qualified human resources to manage these temples. MBAs, diploma or certificate holders in temple management can introduce discipline and organisation in the temple systems. It may also be noted that temples possess a huge employment-generation potential that has not yet been harnessed. Hence, I have included a chapter on temple management.

The chapter on human development is intended to make readers aware of the stages of evolution of human beings. Many people are driven by mental responses and reactions, and they consequently suffer in life. It underlines the human need to use the intellect. If we do this, most of the problems we face in life will be solved.

While many books have been written on Sai Baba, most of them are written from the perspective of bhakti. In this book, I have attempted not only to bring forth some new information but also to give it a practical as well as a spiritual/philosophical touch. It has a beautiful mix of philosophy, spirituality and information. The information presented here is authentic, and you will not be able to find it anywhere else. The book is so written that each chapter is self-standing. You can start reading the book from any chapter.

With the blessings of Baba, I am confident that this book will be very wellreceived by Baba's devotees all over the world. Happy reading.

Om Sairam!

Dr Suresh Haware

ACKNOWLEDGEMENTS

I sincerely acknowledge the help and support received from Mr Praveen Tiwari of Bloomsbury Publishing Plc, Publisher, and thank him for inviting me to write a book on Sai Baba's teachings. This immediately reminded me of my lovely experience of the last five years of being so close to Baba as Chairman of Shri Sai aba Sansthan Trust, Shirdi, and it became the sole cause of my penning the book. The editorial team has taken a lot of interest and made the book almost perfect. I take this opportunity to thank Aerospace Scientist Dr Satheesh Reddy, Chairman, DRDO (Defence Research and Development Organisation), Government of India, for accepting my request and writing the foreword for this book. The photographs are the heart of the book, and I thank the photographers for them. I thank Dr Jeetendra Shelke, Pramod Aher and Mayuri Kadam for providing valuable inputs and also thank Bhagwan Datar, Gayatri Gadgil, Prashant Suryavanshi and Deepak Kate for the editorial help and support extended by them. I thank all my family members, especially my wife Nalini, sons Amit and Amar, daughters-in-law Richa and Ishaanee and grandchildren Aryan, Aaradhya and Ayana.

1. SAI BHAKTI

1

Human Development

Strange paradox in life

There is a strange paradox in life. Whatever experience is pleasurable in the beginning, turns out to be detrimental in the end. And what is detestable in the beginning becomes beneficial, even delightful in the end. Ironically, sorrow appears in the garb of joy and joy appears in the garb of sorrow. As a result, people choose pleasant beginnings only to end in bitterness. And they avoid unpleasant beginnings and lose their joy of life. For example, people do not like to exercise daily; instead they want to be idle and laze around. These choices cause health problems later in life. The human tendency is to grab instant pleasures through undisciplined living and then suffer consequent sorrows. Very few go through the rigours of discipline at the beginning of life and enjoy the peace and happiness it provides later.

This chapter narrates the development of human beings from the historical perspective. It presents the canvas of the stages and steps involved in human development. You can imagine it in the form of a ladder starting from a primitive undeveloped state to the present-day developed state of human beings.

When looking at it from a particular perspective, each one can locate their position on the ladder. Consider that as your starting point leading towards full enlightenment or the realisation of the supreme reality. When such a canvas is available, we can plan our spiritual path of progress accordingly. We must know the destination and the direction. This will help us assess on a regular basis whether we are moving towards the target or away from it.

Living species are broadly classified into three categories, namely plant, animal and human. Plants only have a body and nothing beyond it. They do not have a mind and can therefore not understand love or hate, likes or dislikes and other such emotions. Their existence is limited only to the physical state of being. They cannot move. They do not have choice. However, animals possess both body and mind. They understand emotions. They can move as well. But they do not have much choice. Their behaviour is mostly preprogrammed, in the sense that a cow cannot eat meat and a tiger cannot eat grass. Their lifestyle is almost decided. Though animals have a body and mind, they do not have intellect, which is the distinct quality of human beings. The intellect is the faculty that enables you to think, judge, decide and contemplate. This makes human beings superior than the other two living beings[1]. However, pigeons and dogs are found to have a limited gross intellect. Pigeons can carry the messages over a long distance. They have a sense of location and direction and were used as messengers in both the world wars by military. When all the modes of communication fail, the pigeons are useful.

They are used even today by the French military. Similarly, dogs are used by the military and the police all over the world for tracking, explosive detection, patrol, search, rescue and attack.

Let us learn about the four ages human being has passed through to reach the current developed stage. It is pertinent to learn about human development from the age of perception, age of observation, age of scientific enquiry to the age of contemplation. Though it is difficult to define the historical timeline of these ages, it certainly began thousands of years ago and continues in the present era.

Human beings are made up of body, mind, intellect and spirit. Each of these faculties was not developed initially—they have evolved. It has taken thousands of years for human beings to attain today's position. During the age of perception, human beings would only perceive nature and the happenings around them. They would not act or react. Only the sensory organs (eyes, ears, nose, tongue, skin) were active and the organs of action (mouth, feet, hands, anus, genitals) were passive.

Then came the age of observation. Human beings started observing and correlating the happenings and events around them. For example, if they saw an owl on a particular day when they met with an accident, they correlated these two things to conclude that seeing an owl is inauspicious. They had no knowledge of the science of cause and effect. This science says that every cause has an effect and every effect has a cause. Thus emerged an era of superstitions and rituals, which were proposed as solutions to overcome the negative effects of superstition. At this stage, generation after generation was trapped in superstition and ritualistic practices. This is the phase of sorrow and misery.

They also observed that the sun rose, and they named it morning and defined it as the start of the day. And then that the sun set, so they named it evening, which marks the end of the day. The time of darkness they called night. The sun rose again the next morning and set in the evening. Thus, they discovered the cycle of day and night.

Then came the age of scientific enquiry. Humans began to think. Over a period of time, when humans excelled in their scientific enquiry, they discovered that the sun does not rise, nor does it set. It shines from a fixed location. Day and night happen due to the rotation of the earth around itself. They began to perceive the expressions of cause and effect everywhere and realised that the world is governed by the law of causation. Every cause has an effect and every effect has a cause. In the earlier two ages, i.e. the age of perception and the age of observation, the mind was developed while the intellect remained undeveloped. The awakening of the intellect saw improvement in human beings.

There are some limitations of the mind that one should understand. The mind is restless and governed by likes and dislikes, desires and emotions. You need to control your mind and keep it calm. The mind has to be regulated. An uncontrolled mind can wreck a human being. It plays havoc. Most people succumb to the pressures of the mind, which has proved detrimental, sometimes even fatal, to them. Likes and dislikes are a part of your life. There is nothing fundamentally wrong with them, and you need not avoid them. But do not allow your likes and dislikes to directly propel your actions. You must learn to use reason and judgement to guide you towards enduring peace and happiness.

Unfortunately, humans commit the grave blunder of totally neglecting the intellect. As a result, the human intellect remains unattended and undeveloped. And people become helpless captives of their mind and its devastating attachments. The development of the intellect should commence at an early age, say around seven years. The procedure for the development of the intellect involves two fundamental disciplines. First, do not let your mind take anything for granted, and second, let the intellect question all ideas and accept only those that admit reason and logic. When you follow these two procedures meticulously, the intellect begins to develop[2].

Humans then discovered that the intellect is an instrument to control and guide the mind. The mind behaves like a child while the intellect plays the role of an adult. Just as a child needs constant supervision by an adult, so does the mind need the attention and guidance of the intellect. Initially, the intellect was undeveloped. It developed over a period of time and with the advance of scientific enquiry. People began to enquire into the phenomena of cause and effect, and their enquiry led to the emergence of science. Scientists began to discover the laws governing the world. They started thinking, judging and even making conscious decisions about the happenings around them. Apples fell from trees even before Newton, but only Newton observed the phenomenon, analysed it and discovered the famous law of gravitational forces. This was the beginning of the scientific era.

This is as far as the gross intellect can go. The gross intellect has its own limitations; it has a limited reach. If you want to probe into anything beyond the material world, you need to develop your subtle intellect, which can help comprehend the reality that transcends all scientific enquiry and discovery. Lacking the subtle intellect, humanity remained confined to the scientific era for long years before entering into the age of contemplation.

Following the development of the subtle intellect came the age of contemplation. This is the last stage of human development. Beyond the body and its perceptions and actions, beyond the mind and its impulses and emotions, beyond the intellect and its thoughts lies the higher reality, the God. Human being alone is endowed with the subtle intellect that can contemplate and penetrate into this unknown reality, called 'God' by lay persons. Reaching the transcendental state marks the acme of human existence. Hardly anyone conceives of and much less attempts to attain that state.

The four ages described above follow the gradual development of human beings. However, in today's world, these four stages seem to coexist. There are people at the level of perception alone, if though they are rare. A majority of the people operate based on the impulses of the mind. They are at the observation stage. They are caught up in blind beliefs, superstitions and ritualistic practices. The intellect is virtually absent, and they do not doubt or question their beliefs and superstitions. The vast majority of human beings fall into this category. While there are intellectuals today who have a scientific background, intellectuals having a scientific mindset form a low percentage of them. Rare indeed are those whose thoughts are founded on logic and reason, who will not take things for granted, who will not stop questioning. The modern generation can claim that a very few have reached the age of contemplation, who contemplate reality or God, who revel in the supreme consciousness that pervades the material world. It is difficult to name such persons, but some in the field of spirituality can be believed to be so. The present-day world is, therefore, an admixture of all the four ages of perception, observation, scientific enquiry and contemplation.

I have delved into human development specifically to take you gradually to a discussion of what is required for the spiritual growth of human beings. In order to reach the supreme reality, there is a procedure including meditation to be practised regularly.

Meditation is the art of maintaining the mind in focus upon a chosen thought to the exclusion of all other thought. In the process of meditation, the chant is gradually brought to a mental whisper to finally end in silence. The intellect remains aware of the entire proceeding until the moment of silence is reached. The silence is the cessation of all thought flow, which indicates the extinction of the mind. The intellect, which has been observing the chant, also ceases as there is nothing for it to observe. What remains is pure silence, pure awareness, pure consciousness, the absolute reality. Achieving this state of absolute realisation is the goal of human life[3].

The process of thinking should start from an early age. It is the need of the hour to develop the art of thinking and to follow it up with the study of the truth of life, engage deeply with the truths and apply them in practical life. Adopting this procedure throughout life will enable you to develop your intellect. At the same time, it is also necessary to make full use of the existing intellect. This can be accomplished by the simple daily practice of introspection or self-observation. Do it in this simple way. Every night before going to bed, just sit quietly, close your eyes and try to remember every experience of the day in a sequence, from awakening to the moment of introspection. It may take some time to master this technique, but with time you will be able to recollect each activity. It should not take more than five minutes every day. Take care not to analyse or criticise your actions during introspection, as this might develop cynicism and frustration. Do not get involved; just be an observer. When you remember an action over and over again, you become aware of it. This everyday practice will render your existing intellect more alert.

Let us learn about the strange paradox in life. Whatever experience is pleasurable in the beginning turns out to be detrimental in the end, and what is detestable in the beginning becomes beneficial, even delightful in the end. Ironically, sorrow appears in the garb of joy and joy appears in the garb of sorrow. As a result, people choose pleasant beginnings only to end in bitterness. And they avoid unpleasant beginnings to lose their joy of life. Let us take an example. People do not like to exercise daily; instead, they want be idle and laze around. These choices cause health problems later in life. The human tendency is to grab instant pleasures through undisciplined living and then suffer the consequent sorrows. Very few go through the rigours of discipline at the beginning of life and enjoy the peace and happiness later.

Peer pressure on laypersons pulls them to the lower stages. Those contemplating on the supreme reality are very few. Extreme intellectual effort is required to tear oneself away from such peer pressures and to pursue the highest state of contemplation. Every individual should use their subtle intellect to its maximum capacity to contemplate on and attain the ultimate experience of self-realisation. Now this is the ultimate goal of human beings, the ultimate target. We need to know this and also the path leading to that target. Only then can we decide our movement and its direction.

Now a word of caution. It is a well-known fact that while reading any spiritual or philosophical literature, the phraseology used may differ from that used by another school of spirituality. You need to keep this in mind. The frame of reference used by each is also different. The meaning of the terms may vary. Therefore, the arguments and theories put forth must be read in consonance with the frame of reference. Understanding this is necessary to avoid differences of opinion and to narrow down differences.

I believe that science and spirituality are not competitors; rather, they are complementary to each other. Science deals with the material world, while spirituality deals with the spirit that is beyond the material world. Both have their own separate fields of operation. Both have their own strengths and weaknesses. There is a need to have more and more interaction between these two. Each of them can provide its strength to the other and both of them can grow hand in hand.

2

Sai Bhakti

> **Bhakti is complete surrender to God**
>
> *Usually it is accepted that the characteristic feature of the religious development during the medieval period was single-minded and solely based on intense devotion to God. It was a complete surrender of oneself to God. This was the Bhakti Movement—the movement that emphasised devotion to God. Bhakti was accepted as salvation.*

Bhakti is nothing but devotion and love. It is one of the intrinsic aspects of human nature. Bhakti has been an inseparable part of Indian society. Sai Bhakti, as an experience, is deeply rooted in the hearts of Sai devotees. Devotees have unquestionable faith in Sai Baba. Expressions of this faith are manifested in the temple time and time again. Though bhakti is related to the individual and is adopted as a method of salvation, there was an organised movement called the Bhakti Movement that became one of the biggest public movements in India.

Usually it is accepted that the characteristic feature of religious development during the medieval period was the movement that emphasised single-minded devotion to God. It was a complete surrender of oneself to God. This was the Bhakti Movement—devotion to God[4]. Bhakti was accepted as a path to salvation.

The main features of the Bhakti Movement are as follows:

1. Unity of God or one God known by different names
2. Bhakti, intense love and devotion, the only way to salvation
3. Chanting of the name of God
4. Self-surrender
5. Condemnation of superstitions and blind faith
6. Open-mindedness about deciding religious matters
7. No distinction between different castes
8. Need of a guru for guidance advocated by some
9. Preaching through local or regional languages and travelling from place to place to spread the religious message

Devotion and love are two forms of the same emotion. They differ only in direction. When your emotion flows towards a lower object or being, it is called 'love'. You love your children, your pets, your home. When you direct the same emotion towards a higher being, it becomes 'devotion'. You are devoted to your parents, to your guru, to God. Between the beings at the same level, it could be a mixture of love and devotion. Devotion is not something that one can pass on to another. It has to be cultivated through your own efforts. The 35 gunas or values help you develop devotion to God.

Thirty-five Qualities of a True Devotee (Bhakta)

Many doctrines of bhakti may be found in the Bhagawad Gita, in which Lord Krishna specifies 35 qualities of a bhakta in Chapter XII of the last portion. He deems those possessing these qualities as His true devotees. Devotion to God is not blind faith, mere prayer or routine ritual. True devotion comprises these outstanding qualities. It also envisages conscious effort to instil these values in one's practical life. Lord Krishna affirms that those living these qualities are exceedingly dear to Him.

The 35 qualities of a true devotee or bhakta that are mentioned in the verses 13 to 20 of Chapter XII of the Bhagawad Gita are given below[5,6]:

1. Not hating any being
2. Friendliness
3. Compassion
4. Freedom from attachment
5. Freedom from egoism
6. Balance in pleasure and pain
7. Forgiveness
8. Contentment
9. Yog (uniting with the Self)
10. Self-control
11. A firm conviction
12. Surrender of the mind and intellect to God
13. By whom the world is not agitated
14. Calmness when faced with the world
15. Absence of joy, envy, fear and anxiety
16. Absence of desire

17. Purity
18. Competence in action
19. Indifference
20. Freedom from anxiety
21. Renunciation of the fruits of action
22. Absence of elation, hatred, fear
23. Absence of grief
24. Renunciation of good and evil
25. Equal-mindedness towards friends and enemies
26. Equanimity in honour and dishonour
27. Equanimity in heat and cold or success and failure
28. Equanimity in joy and sorrow
29. Non-attachment
30. Equal-mindedness in praise and blame
31. Silence
32. Contentment with whatsoever is obtained by chance
33. Absence of attachment to the home
34. Firmness in decisions
35. Devotion to God

The real development of bhakti took place in South India between the 7th and the 12th centuries through the teachings of poet saints known as Alvars and Nayanars, whose hymns were collected and compiled in the 10th century. The spiritual yearning made Kabir, Guru Nanak, Mirabai, Surdas, Tulsidas, Chaitanya and others the great exponents of the Bhakti Movement[5].

The main principles of the Bhakti Movement were (1) God is one, (2) to worship God, people should serve *humanity*, (3) all men are equal, (4) worshipping God with devotion is better than performing religious ceremonies and going on pilgrimages and (5) caste distinctions and superstitious practices are to be given up[7].

You get what you deserve and not what you desire. You are the creator of your destiny. Your future lies in your hand. You can make or mar your fortune. Therefore, the actions in the present should be carefully chosen, as each one of them will contribute to the future. You must also have heard about navavidha bhakti.

Navavidha Bhakti

Srimad Bhagavatam describes nine forms of bhakti which, if cultivated and practised regularly, will no doubt lead us closer to the Lord: shravanam, kirtanam, smaranam, paada-sevanam, archanam, vandanam, daasyam, sakhyam, aatma-nivedanam (Srimad Bhagavatam 7.5.23).

The nine forms of devotion are as follows:

1. Shravanam: hearing the names and glories of the Lord
2. Keertanam: chanting His glories
3. Smaranam: remembering the Lord
4. Paada sevanam: serving the Lord's feet
5. Archanam: worshipping the Lord
6. Vandanam: offering obeisance unto the Lord
7. Daasyam: serving the Lord as His servant
8. Sakhyam: developing friendship with the Lord
9. Aatma Nivedanam: total surrender of oneself to the Lord.

Hearing the Lord's stories, Parikshit attained Him; Vyasa's son attained Him by singing His glories, Prahlada by constantly remembering Him, Lakshmi by serving at His feet, Prithu by worshipping Him, Akrura by adoring Him, Hanuman by being His humble servant, Bali by being His friend and dedicating his all to Him—these are the nine ways of attaining Him. All attained salvation equally, though by different methods[8].

Let us try to understand the role of bhakti in the scientific and rational process of attaining salvation. Vasanas, which manifest as thoughts and desires in human beings, differentiate them from the supreme reality or God. Uproot your desires, vasanas and thoughts, and you become one with God. Yoga is the technique to unite yourself with God. The shastras have prescribed many yogas for the eradication of the vasanas. For example, Bhakti Yoga, which is the path of devotion, is suitable for emotional people; Gnana Yoga, which is the path of knowledge, is suitable for intellectual people; Karma Yoga, which is the path of action, is suitable for active people; Hatha Yoga, which is the path of compulsion, is suitable for not-so-active people. These disciplines are specially designed to suit the distinct categories of people classified according to their inner nature. Their nature depends upon the relative strengths of their mind and intellect. Following the respective discipline, an aspirant can gradually reduce their desires and prepare themselves for meditation leading to the ultimate state of self-realisation[3].

In emotional people, the mind is more pronounced than the intellect. Such a person's heart dominates over their head. When given the choice of 'dil se' or 'dimag se', they will choose to act 'dil se'. Such a person is more impulsive, emotional, devotional, less rational, less intellectual and less contemplative. They give in to their feelings and emotion. Their mind rules their personality. Such a person is designed for the path of devotion, Bhakti Yoga. They need a form, an image of the Supreme that matches with their emotions and devotion. Their mind revels in the remembrance of the Lord of their heart. Devotion to the Lord displaces all other feelings and thoughts. Consequently, their mind is focused upon the higher. With sustained devotion, the devotee becomes free of their desires.

The second type of person is the intellectual, whose intellect is more developed than their mind. They are more analytical and rational and less impulsive and emotional. Their intellect controls the passion of their mind. Their head predominates over their heart. 'Dil se nahi, dimag se' is their personality type. They remain objective and do not succumb to their feelings and emotion. They are logical in their approach to life. They are seekers and perceive the distinction between the terrestrial and the transcendental. They will not be satisfied in merely postulating or worshipping an idol like the emotional person. They do not take things for granted, but need logic and reason to accept anything. A person of such personality is suited for the path of knowledge, Gnana Yoga. Following this path, they become immersed in the contemplation of the supreme reality. Consequently, their thoughts and desires gradually cease to exist.

The third type of person, classified as active, possesses a mind and intellect more or less equally developed. They switch between moods, being sometimes rational and at other times emotional, and have a mixed temperament. Karma Yoga, the path of action, is suitable for such a person, where both mind and intellect are engaged. The mind surrenders to the higher ideals they work for while the intellect channels action towards that ideal. Thus, with the mind and intellect set on the higher goal, they shed their worldly thoughts and desires.

The fourth category is of the not-so-active person. Their intellect is relatively less developed and it is difficult for them to conceive of the existence of transcendental reality. Understanding spirituality through either the mind or the intellect or a combination of both is also difficult. The only recourse left to them is to administer discipline forcibly through the physical body following the path of compulsion, Hatha Yoga. 'Hatha' means force. Thus, Hatha Yoga is a comprehensive discipline and is administered through force. It covers a schedule of physical exercises known as asana and pranayama and a series of other practices involving self-exertion. These practices help to draw the practitioner out of their inaction and help in the development of the mind and intellect. They slowly evolve and gradually grow to qualify for the other three spiritual courses. It is not that the nature of a person does not change throughout their life. Human nature is highly adaptable and can change depending upon the circumstances and the environment the person is living in. It can elevate or it can degrade. The different forms of yoga could be interchangeable depending upon the changes in the nature of a person. There could also be more categories of persons and more forms of yoga suitable for them. A general description is given above and should be used as a guiding principle.

The different categories of human beings only indicate the preponderance of their respective nature. No one is wholly intellectual or emotional or wholly lacking in emotion or reason. Hence, in each category, we find a dominant portion of their respective nature with minor aspects of the other three. An aspirant has to primarily analyse and assess the proportions constituting their own nature before they choose their spiritual discipline. Thereafter, they need to proportion the four paths of yoga to suit their composite nature. Thus, the one categorised as intellectual will primarily need Gnana Yoga along with portions of other three paths to meet the needs of the remaining aspects of their nature. So do the emotional and active persons need to concentrate mainly on their respective yoga and to proportionately combine it with the other paths, while the not-so-active person has to plunge into Hatha Yoga with traces of the other three disciplines. If an aspirant follows this methodical procedure, their spiritual development will be meteoric.

Thus, with regular practice of yoga, the mind gets rid of all desires except the ultimate desire for self-realisation. It no longer rushes to the outer world—rather, it turns inwards. An introverted mind is alone qualified to meditate and attain spiritual enlightenment.

3

Sai Leela

Manifestation of His divine powers

Sai Leela refers to the manifestations of His divine powers such as the burning of oil lamps with water when a shopkeeper refused to give Him oil, His curing/ healing of patients and safeguarding the town from an epidemic. All these are considered His miracles. There may be some logic, reason or science behind each of His acts.

Sai philosophy has two prominent aspects, namely Sai Leela and Sai Seva. Devotees are more familiar with Sai Leela, but Sai Seva is more pronounced in His teachings through daily practices. Special chapters in this book are devoted to a detailed discussion of each.

Sai Leela refers to the manifestations of His divine powers. For example, when a shopkeeper refused to give Him oil, He put water instead in the lamps and lighted them without oil. He cured/healed the patients with treatment and, at times, with his divine power, he safeguarded the town from an epidemic. He even gave darshan to devotees in the form of Vitthal of Pandharpur. All these are considered His miracles. There may be some logic, reason or science behind each of His acts. However, no one has tried to analyse them. Most devotees believe in these mystic events, love them and admire them. Rarely are they open to scrutiny, whether scientific or otherwise. Devotees strongly believe that He possessed extraordinary power.

Sai Baba need not always exist in the physical form. He could exist in other forms that do not have the limitations of a physical body. He could be here and at the same time, He could be far away. With only His words of promise, He could cure patients near Him or even far away from Him. His devotees have experienced this, and you will find plenty of such experiences in the *Shri Sai Satcharitra*[9] written by Govind Raghunath Dabholkar, which is considered to be the only authentic book on Sai Baba. These stories are not just hearsay but are true incidents with actual witnesses. I will narrate a few such stories, all of them taken from *Shri Sai Satcharitra*, for the sake of completeness of the book and for the information of the readers.

In 1911, a lamb came in front of Dwarkamai in a dying condition. Very soon, it fell down and stopped moving, lying as if dead. Everyone present rushed to the scene, but they were all helpless. They requested Baba to do something and save the lamb. Baba approached the lamb, held it close and gave it some water. In no time, it started jumping and ran to its mother.

Baba cured many patients by giving them udi prasad. He cured the eyes of a patient in a village using a marking nut, which is unusual but true. He cured Kakasaheb Mahajani of his dysentery by asking him to eat some groundnuts; this may appear illogical but is reported to be true. Baba cured Dr Pilley of dracunculiasis, also called Guinea-worm disease, by simply giving him udi. He advised Bala Shimpi to feed dogs, and Shimpi was cured of his malaria.

Baba would sleep on a wooden plank hung from the roof of Dwarkamai with the help of a weak cloth. Nobody saw him either climbing up onto the plank or climbing down from it. The devotees wondered how the weak cloth tied up between the plank and the roof of Dwarakamai could bear His weight, but many people witnessed him sleeping on it. Devotees consider this as Baba's leela.

It is also reported that Baba would cure devotees who lived a long distance away, perhaps like modern telemedicine. The daughter of Nanasaheb Chandorkar, a staunch devotee of Baba, was undergoing unbearable labour pain. Baba administered her udi from a long distance away and relieved her pain. Once he promised to visit Balasaheb Deo at his house in Dhule, which is far away from Shirdi. He did so without leaving Shirdi. Another time he visited a devotee's house in Bandra, again without leaving Shirdi. There, he did not get any food as nobody recognised him and hence nobody bothered about Him. And so He had to return hungry. He entered Megha's (a devotee's) house without opening any of the doors.

Baba gave darshan to some of his devotees in the form of their gurus. This could be an example of 'par kaya pravesh' or transmigration of a living soul. Once Dasganu Maharaj wished to see Vitthal without going to Pandharpur, and Baba fulfilled his wish by giving him darshan in the form of Vitthal. Again, Dasganu wished to go to Prayag Tirth, where the three holy rivers Ganga, Yamuna and Saraswati meet, and to take holy baths at the sangam. Baba said to him, 'Why do you need to go so far? See, here are the rivers Ganga and Yamuna.' The waters started flowing from the toes of Sai Baba. One Mr Muley was staying at Nashik, a city at a distance of around 100 km from Shirdi. Baba gave him darshan in the form of Gholapswami, his guru, who had taken samadhi long ago. When a lady devotee came from Chennai to Shirdi for Baba's darshan, he gave her darshan in the form of Shri Ram, whom she loved very much. Once Mrs Tarkhad fed a dog. Baba told her that he was happy as she had given him food. On being questioned, he said, 'Sometimes I'm a dog, sometimes a cow and sometimes another animal.' Baba asked Laxmibai of Shirdi to get him food. When she brought it, he fed it to a dog and told her, 'He is me and I am he.'

Such are the ways of Baba. Sai devotees believe that if you surrender to Him with complete faith and devotion, He will provide you succour and fulfil your wish even now, though He is no longer with us physically. Baba has made 11 promises to His devotees, assuring them that He will take care of them even if He cannot be present physically. It is said that faith has the strength to move mountains.

I have not scrutinised these events and happenings as they have been reported responsibly in an authentic and respected source[9]. I am aware that there is no basis for such mystic happenings in science, but they cannot be brushed aside since they have witnesses. There has been no scientific investigation of such events either. Sometimes, one has to believe that science has its own limitations and there is something beyond it.

4

Shraddha

Shraddha is faith with devotion and love

Shraddha cannot be equated directly with faith. Faith is a very small word to describe shraddha. We can say shraddha is faith imbued with devotion and love. Shraddha is a very important aspect of the human mindset. We observe that when a person needs healthcare, he consults that doctor only in whom he has shraddha. So also when he chooses a goldsmith or a grocer. We go to only those places that inspire faith.

Shri Sai Baba has not left behind any written text, unlike many other saints. Sant Dnyaneshwar wrote the *Dnyaneshwari*, Sikh Gurus from Guru Nanak to Guru Govind Singh Guru wrote the *Granth Sahib* and so on. *Shri Sai Satcharitra*, though not written by Sai Baba himself, was written by Govind Raghunath Dabholkar with the blessings of Baba and is thus the authentic book on Him. Baba propagated His philosophy through direct discourse with devotees and succeeded in conveying it to each and every person in a very simple manner. His ideals of shraddha and saburi became a powerful mantra for everyone. Each word has a deep meaning and an impact on human behaviour. Both aspects are equally necessary. Let us discuss shraddha first.

Shraddha cannot be directly equated with faith, which is a very small word to describe shraddha. We can say shraddha is faith imbued with devotion and love. Shraddha is a very important aspect of the human mindset. We observe that when we need healthcare, we consult only that doctor in whom we have shraddha. So also when we choose a goldsmith or grocer. We go to only those places that inspire faith. When we board a flight, we have faith in the airlines and their pilot, though we do not know them personally. When we take admission to a particular school or college, we have faith in that institution, even though we do not personally know the chairman or trustees. Thus, faith is not just a word but a deep-rooted experience that helps us decide. Shraddha is the basic foundation for human beings. If the foundation is strong, you can build a tall building on it and not otherwise. Shraddha builds your confidence and is, therefore, a necessary ingredient of the human personality.

Shraddha is the strongest and highest power in moulding one's life in a specific direction. The essence of shraddha is unshakable belief in noble ideals. When this belief in high principles becomes a practice and a part of life, it is called devotion; when this matured belief becomes a realisation of the self and of God, it is called siddhi. Despite following the same mantra, the same method of sadhana and the guidance of the same guru, the spiritual unfolding of different sadhaks progresses at a different pace. Some sadhaks climb the steps of self-realisation quickly while others appear to crawl. The reason is that when it comes to spirituality, the power of shraddha is supreme. As it is possible to perform heavy physical activities and accomplish difficult tasks with strong muscle power, so the power of shraddha enables us to work beyond our capacity and get surprising results[10].

It is faith that transforms lifeless stones into living symbols of divinity with supernatural powers. At the time of building the Ram Setu to Sri Lanka, the stones thrown by Reechha and Vanar (creatures of the class of bear and monkey) with deep devotion towards Lord Ram floated on water, but the stones that were thrown by Ram himself did not float. It is faith that produces supernatural powers. The great seer Patanjali has explained that even the normal devotees can achieve samadhi on the basis of shraddha.

Shraddha makes the common person uncommon and also the other way around. If you go to a doctor and do not have shraddha, you will question their every action. You will not have faith in the medicine or the treatment they have prescribed. You may not follow it scrupulously and may not get the desired results.

A great saint by the name of Manickavasagar said, 'Lord, You know what I want. And You will give me everything that I need. If by any chance, with my own little egoistic self, I feel that I want something, I should know that even that want is created by You. Without You, I wouldn't even have a want. If it is my want, it will never get fulfilled. So I leave it to You. You give me whatever I need for Your service. The minute You think that I have finished with that tool and I don't need it anymore, take it away.' It all boils down to this one thing: faith in a higher power, an unseen hand that constantly moulds us. 'You put me here, I am here. You gave me this job, I am doing it.' There's no superiority or inferiority. No 'How come he is doing that, while I am doing this?' No. God selects each one for work and gives various jobs to various people. Everything is equally great. There is nothing superior or inferior. Do every job joyfully as God's work. In the process of working, if your mind goes through some turmoil, suspicion or doubt, it will get cleared up when you meditate. All the problems that you created in your doing are undone by meditating. That's why meditation is so important[11].

The mantra shraddha-saburi generates boundless positive energy, enabling one to withstand seemingly insurmountable adversities. I have failed to find a word in English expressing the subtle emotion that 'shraddha' conveys to Hindus. The expression 'unshakable reverential faith' might colloquially suggest a broader meaning, yet it too misses the deeper and subtle importance of shraddha.

Shraddha and saburi are interwoven and inseparable. Shraddha engenders an unqualified sense of surrender to the omnipotent and omnipresent triple Divine Force i.e. 'will', 'wisdom' and 'action'. When with the Divine inspiration we are freed of egoistic and egocentric will, wisdom and action, we are automatically freed of the desire for the fruits of action. Saburi thus emerges effortlessly.

Outwardly, though we continue to remain engaged in ostensible worldly pursuits, peace prevails within. We become just the witness of ubiquitous, all-pervading spectacles of cause and effect while remaining detached.

Human joy and sorrow invariably flow from the sense of egoistic agency. Egocentric agency inescapably leads to joy if the action produces expected results and to sorrow, if it doesn't. Thus the egocentric doer remains stuck in the endless cycle of joy and sorrow, both ephemeral. The endless cycle of now-joy–now-sorrow ultimately leads to a state of frustration and misery. No amount of material wealth can help you escape this fate. Even those who have all the material resources at their disposal are found suffering from such mental/physical ailments that they tend to commit suicide.

Bliss is the essential nature of human beings. It's the natural quest for bliss that mistakenly finds satisfaction, albeit momentarily, in the joy that the expected fruits of egoistic actions produce, only to be followed by sorrow the very next moment when they fail to do so.

It is only when guided by the Divine grace that one arrives at the highest plane of shraddha (unqualified reverential surrender to the Divine Will) and that the unalloyed and inexhaustible patience (saburi) is born, leading to eternal Bliss, Sachidananda[12].

Spirituality is a field that demands unquestionable faith, and that has to come from within. Your inner voice should speak of that. The rewards of unquestionable faith are manifold in spirituality. Therefore, shraddha is an essential component of a human being, whatever the field you are working in. Even science needs faith, and scientists also need shraddha. With faith, they can perform what would be impossible without faith. Faith makes you stable, sturdy, confident and unshakable. If you want to be successful in life, you cannot achieve it without shraddha. That is the importance of shraddha in human life. So have shraddha, and keep testing it through your experiences until you achieve complete faith. The rewards will be miraculous.

Shraddha
means you have peace
even when you don't have all the answers.

5

Saburi

Saburi is patience with devotion and love

Once, I went to the famous Siddhivinayak temple at Prabhadevi, Mumbai. I found a mouse made of silver in the temple premises, and devotees were telling their sorrows into the ears of this silver mouse. There was a queue before the mouse as devotees waited to share their story with the mouse. They believed that the mouse was the messenger of Lord Ganesha and would take their sorrows directly to the Lord. This is somewhat similar to the confession service available in religious centres. In response to the popular demand by devotees, the temple management decided to place four such silver mice in the temple premises, and all of them are now busy listening to the worries of the devotees.

Saburi, I believe, is much more important than shraddha. It is not merely patience; it implies an element of devotion too. Saburi is then patience imbued with devotion and love. The lack of saburi is the root of most human problems. If you listen to someone patiently, 90 per cent of their problem is resolved then and there. People need patient listening. It may be noted here that listening is an art and must be employed properly. It is only with practice that you can master this art over a period of time. Many people and even institutions have realised this need. I have already narrated my experience at Mumbai's Siddhivinayak temple, which has ultimately placed four mice in the premises to listen to the devotee's grievances.

Irrespective of whether there is any science behind this happening, it is clear that listening is a necessity. This need results from the increasing lack of saburi in society. Most people give up before they receive the fruit; only the one who is patient succeeds. Saburi does not come naturally; it has to be learned. If you give it enough time, any wound can be healed, any anger soothed, any enmity pacified, any fire extinguished, any ocean crossed and any mountain scaled. All you need is saburi.

Look at the scale of impact saburi has on human beings. You will also realise that the benefits it offers are manifold.

The teachings of Sai Baba have inspired many to be aware of the limits of the mortal body. He asked devotees for complete surrender to the guru. He led by example to teach the importance of compassion to his disciples. Shraddha and saburi are the cardinal principles to walk on the Sai path. Saburi, He says, has patience and perseverance. It is an important quality that anyone walking on the path of salvation needs. Without saburi, a seeker may leave the path midway[13].

The *Katha Upanishad* recounts a very interesting story of the young and virtuous Nachiketa. It begins with a description of the atma, as follows:

- To very few is it given to hear about the atma.
- Many more who hear of the atma do not understand it.

- Wonderful is the person who speaks of it.
- Intelligent is the person who learns of it.
- Most blessed is he who learns it from a guru and understands it.

When the Nachiketa's father gives away inferior gifts as part of a ritual ceremony, the boy tries to lessen the impact of this serious error in judgement. The father gets angry and disgusted at his interference and shouts that he is going to give the son away to Yama, the god of death. The son resolves that the words uttered by the father should not be untrue, so he proceeds to the residence of Yama to offer himself up as a ritualistic gift. The boy spends three nights waiting to see Yama. When Yama discovers his presence, he feels sorry that the boy had to wait so long, so he decides to grant him three boons, one for each night he waited.

Nachiketa asks first that when he returns home, his father will have shed his anger and gained mental equanimity and so welcome him home. Second, he asks to know the secret of the absence of hunger and fear of death in the heavenly worlds. Yama gladly grants these boons and further initiates his new disciple into the details of a special ritual ceremony.

Yama sees the reverence, intelligence, and eagerness of his new pupil and is much pleased with him. Nachiketa then asks for his third boon. He tells his new teacher, 'Some say that death is not the end; that there is an entity called the atma which survives the body and senses. Teach me that secret of the atma.'

Yama at first resists and decides to test him to see if he is deserving of this unique knowledge. He offers him many other attractive boons involving worldly prosperity and happiness. But Nachiketa firmly declines these ephemeral favours. 'The alternative boons you hold before me cannot assure me the everlasting benefit that atmagnana (knowledge of the atma) alone can bestow.' Yama is again pleased with his pupil and deems him fit to receive the highest wisdom. The remainder of the Upanishad contains his teachings to Nachiketa. The young disciple grasps the teachings immediately and thoroughly, and putting them into practice, he attains the Brahma at the age of 14. Yama tested his saburi and rewarded him.

'Patience is a spiritual movement in which one allows the timing of events to run at its own pace and course and does not prematurely interfere.' Patience thus reflects the Witness Consciousness of the Infinite Divine, its Stillness, Beingness and Truth extended to the field of life. Haste, its opposite, attracts difficulty and opposition, as one is out of phase with the true unfolding and flow of one's existence. Patience, like kindness, is a quality that characterises the spiritual life from beginning to end. But it too takes on different nuances as one gets some years under one's belt and begins settling in for the long run. Patience fades gradually into tranquillity. One begins to understand that the means and the ends cannot be different, that to 'reach' the goal we simply must practice it here and now. As a bestselling American author and teacher in the Vipassana movement in America, Jack Kornfield writes in relation to patience, 'In the deepest way it understands that what we seek is what we are, and it is always here.'

The Italian spiritual writer, Carlo Carretto, after spending more than 20 years in solitude as a monk in the Sahara Desert, was asked what single thing he felt that he heard God say to him inside the long, deep silence. What, he was asked, do you hear God saying to the world? His answer: God is asking us to wait, to be patient!

Why the need for such great patience? Does God want to test us? Does God want to see if we indeed have faith that is worthy of a great reward? No. God has no need to play such a game, and neither do we. It is not that God wants to test our patience. The need for patience arises out of the rhythms innate within life and within love.

What is time? What does it mean when we say that time has gone by, when we want to tell something about the past? And when we have to say something about the future, we say that the time is yet to come. Now the question is, where has the time gone? Similarly, if it is yet to come, from where will it come? Does time move back and forth, or do we move back and forth against the time scale? Perhaps the time scale is stable like a road and we move along it. Or perhaps we are stable like a tree, and time moves like a bus moving on the road. We can add our imagination into the thinking process. I think time doesn't move. It is stationary, unlike the clock, and we move back and forth. Patience is all about running against time. It is a great teacher and all our successes and failures in life are decided by this single force—patience.

One of the simplest attitudes towards time is based on whether we are patient or impatient. If we are willing to accept the duration of time required to accomplish a thing or for a matter to unfold, then we are of a patient disposition. That patience is founded on a calm vital faith that all will unfold in its right sequence and in due time. Through such poise, life constantly cooperates without effort, generating the greatest results in the shortest period of time. On the other hand, when we are reactive and hurried, we create an imbalance of energies that not only retards practical, positive results, but may align with problematic circumstances. We may experience this as ill-fortune. The result will be that life will quickly cancel the opening, turning our joy into regret and sorrow. Thus, anyone who is of an impatient bent is advised to change that quality immediately to avoid such damaging outcomes in the future.

> 'With time and patience the mulberry leaf becomes a silk gown.'

Patience is the space between your dreams and their manifestation. It's a gentle knowing and a deep trust that all good things come in time, and that challenging times eventually pass. Patience requires awareness, acceptance and allowing: awareness of not only the goal, but also of the bigger picture; acceptance of the ebb and flow of pieces coming together and allowing the process to unfold in its own time[15].

In a recent study, people were asked to choose between winning a small prize immediately and larger prizes that they would have to wait several weeks to claim. Perhaps unsurprisingly, 70 per cent chose the smaller prize.

But follow-up questioning revealed that those who chose to wait treasured their rewards more than those who claimed their prize immediately—even in cases where the prizes were identical. And researchers found another reason to opt out of instant gratification: they noticed that the act of waiting itself actually increases our capacity for patience.

These days, technology may have rendered the need to wait as obsolete; but patience, as both a rational and a spiritual practice, holds hidden treasures: willpower, anticipation, gratitude, appreciation, faith.

'Patience and self-control are key factors in achieving success across every aspect of our life, including school, career, health, and relationships', says University of Chicago business professor Ayelet Fishbach, who led a study on the subject. 'The reason is that patient people can delay gratification, control their impulse, and go for the larger prize, which is the key to many successful outcomes[16].'

How can you strengthen your patience? Try these tips:

- Incorporate waiting periods into every selection process, even if you can choose immediately. Fishbach advises: 'Basically, don't make your decision right away. Wait for a while and you'll discover that you've got better self-control.'
- Try thinking of patience as a gift you give to yourself and others. If good things come to those who wait,

imagine the joy of sharing your success with your loved ones when it comes to pass.

- Turn waiting into a practice. Open your awareness: how does waiting feel in the body, mind and spirit? Learn to recognise and welcome it as you would a friendly challenge.
- Turn waiting into a game. 'Just thinking about how long you've been waiting could be enough to increase your patience and self-control,' Fishbach says. The self-confidence boost from 'Hey, I've held out for a whole week!' can make you feel like a strong winner.

Saburi
is not about how long you can wait,
but how well you behave while you're waiting.

6

Seva

Seva is a prominent aspect of Sai Baba's teachings

He would pick up a broom and would Himself clean the temple premises every day. His motive was to ensure cleanliness. He would plant trees and water them every day; the basic thought behind this act was environmental care. He would care for cows and animals. He would Himself nurse the patients and would take all the medical care to cure them. Healthcare was the motive behind this action. Every action of his was a service towards society and humanity; we can call it Sai Seva.

Sai Baba used to ask for bhiksha at five houses in Shirdi every day. That would be His staple for the day for Himself and the devotees. Begging or alms are not proper translations of bhiksha, as bhiksha involves giving up the ego. Thus there is an element of devotion in it. It can be called devotional begging. He would grind the grains received as bhiksha and cook the food Himself. He would serve it to the devotees and only then would he consume it Himself. He would also feed dogs, cats, cows, other animals and birds. He would take care of all creatures. He would say, just as you have hunger, the animals and birds also get hungry.

The leftover food of the day would be kept in Dwarkamai, and anybody could come and eat it. Even today, if you go to Shirdi and visit Dwarkamai, you will find a jute sack full of wheat kept there. The grinder He used then can also be seen there today. Annadan was His motive. Sai Baba Sansthan Shirdi has a mega kitchen (described in a special chapter in the latter part of this book) which feeds around a lakh devotees every day, free of cost. Annadan is one of the core activities of the temple. Devotees visiting Shirdi also donate funds for annadan in the name of their near and dear ones.

Baba would pick up a broom and would Himself clean the premises every day, immediately after He woke and performed his ablutions. This was his daily routine. The devotees also participated in His cleanliness movement. Cleanliness creates a healthy atmosphere. If you spend one-tenth of the amount on cleanliness that you spend on healthcare, you will be saved from all health issues.

Sai Baba always led by example. He did not merely deliver lectures on cleanliness or other subjects. Practical implementation was his way of teaching, that too with the principle of first person singular. He would begin an activity first and then others would follow Him.

Baba planted trees and watered them every day. The Lendi Baug that you see in the temple premises now is His creation. He visited the adjoining villages and brought plants from there and then planted them in the Lendi Baug. He would fetch water from the well and carry it in earthenware pots to water the trees. Even today, the Lendi Baug boasts trees that were planted by Sai Baba Himself. Human beings require oxygen for survival. And there is no producer of oxygen other than trees, which do so naturally, without human intervention or effort, and even consume unwanted carbon dioxide. Imagine a world with no trees—carbon dioxide would fill the atmosphere and oxygen would be depleted. The planet would soon be unliveable. The amount of oxygen produced by an acre of trees per year equals the amount consumed by 18 people annually. One tree produces nearly 118 kg of oxygen each year. One acre of trees removes up to 2.6 tonnes of carbon dioxide each year[17]. Baba taught us the importance of trees and environmental care. So environmental care was the basic thought behind his actions.

Baba would care for cows and animals. He not only fed them but also nursed them Himself, treating them as he would treat human beings. He cared for birds too. There is a memorial statue of a tiger in front of the Shiva temple inside the Sai Baba Temple premises at Shirdi. Baba provided succour to the tiger and set him free. As narrated in the *Sai Satcharitra*, the tiger was still tied up to its karma or its deeds of its previous birth. With Baba's blessings, it was set free. The moment Baba released it, it walked a few steps and took its last breath on the steps of Dwarakamai.

Baba used to organise bhajan and kirtan; these were his favourite activities and would take place frequently in the temple. The folk art form called 'tamasha' was very popular then. It would be performed in Shirdi for the purpose of entertainment. Such cultural activities were organised in the temple on the occasion of festivals. Today, a special mandap has been created in the 16 gunthas of land adjoining the temple, where social and cultural activities can be organised every day. Baba always encouraged cultural activities.

Baba also promoted sports. He used to wrestle and would organise wrestling matches every year in Shirdi.

He would nurse patients Himself and would take all the medical care to cure them. Healthcare was very close to His heart. Baba treated hundreds of patients. *Shri Sai Satcharitra* narrates instances of Him providing medical care on almost every page. There are instances where He cured patients who were at distant places, while remaining physically present in Shirdi. This is a form of telemedicine. In His memory, Sai Baba Sansthan has set up two large hospitals with a total capacity of 575 beds (this is described in detail in the latter chapter in this book). Healthcare was a motive behind His actions.

Baba would play with children and impart good values to educate them. Education lay at the base of His playfulness.

Broadly speaking, service can be categorised into three types—selfish, unselfish and selfless service. Most people perform selfish service—they look for personal benefit. Very few perform unselfish service, without a prominent selfish motive, yet they do not care for the beneficiary. In the third and most important category, selfless service, the personal benefit is not at all considered—the beneficiary is the focus of the action. The welfare of the beneficiary is the most important[3]. The service or seva that we discuss with reference to Sai Baba is selfless service. His life is an example of this.

Many of His actions were aimed at service towards society. We can call it Sai Seva. Here, again, I shall draw your attention to the meaning of seva. It is not mere service, rather service with devotion and love. I deeply feel that the manifestations of His Sai Leela were also partly for the purpose of Seva. As much as Sai Baba is remembered for Sai Leela, so should He be remembered for Sai Seva.

7

Sab ka Mailk Ek

Universal statement by Sai Baba

'Ekam sat vipra bahudha vadanti' is a main sutra (theme) quote from the Upanishads. This aphorism means, 'That which exists is ONE, sages called it by various names.' This idea from the Upanishads has been ingrained in Indian civilisation for thousands of years, resulting in the extreme tolerance practised by Hindus on the whole. Jains and Buddhists emphasise the idea of coexistence and tolerance as well. This idea was further expanded in urging the masses to see His presence, God's presence, in every atom of the universe; and this implied the presence of the same One soul in all living things. In the Bhagwad Gita, it was most emphatically stressed when Lord Krishna tells Arjuna that the soul is immortal.

'Sab ka mailk ek' is a universal teaching of Sai Baba. It is a universally accepted truth that God is one; people view God differently. All spiritual schools of thought express this idea. There are differences in the words of prayer spoken, in the holy symbols used and the rituals practised, but the underlying principle is the same, i.e. 'sab ka mailk ek'.

The Shrimad Bhagwad Gita propagates the universality of God. The idea of the oneness of God is reflected in these words, 'Even those devotees who worship other gods worship Me alone' (Bhagwad Gita, IX: 23). It is not the manner of worship but the love of a selfless devotee of pure heart that matters, because 'Whoever offers to me with devotion, a leaf, a flower, a fruit, or water ... I accept' (Bhagwad Gita, IX: 26).

Sab ka (of all the creatures) malik (lord) ek (only one). The sentence conveys the meaning that there is only one Lord of all creatures. The Narayan Upanishad says that whatever in this world you see or hear of, Narayan (Lord) is present there (meaning that he is omnipresent). In Guru Granth Sahib, He has been described as 'Sat Kartar' (True Doer or Operator), which implies that He is omnipotent. Sai Baba also preached the same truth: that this Lord is eternal, perfect, indivisible, omnipresent and omnipotent. He lords over the activities of the entire universe. This is what Adi Shankaracharya told us about Advait Brahm: 'Eko brahm dwiteeyo naasti' ('There is only one Brahm, not any other')[18].

'Sab ka mailk ek' ('There is only one God who governs all') is one of the most popular phrases I have come across right from my childhood. I personally believe in this saying. Every one of us may have heard this somewhere or the other, but most do not know from where this got originated. Shirdi Sai Baba is the answer. He is one of those who popularised this idea with the intention of taking everybody on a righteous path and of eliminating/curbing any differences or discrimination. Shirdi Sai Baba, also known as Sai Baba or Sai Nath or Shirdiwale Sai Baba, is a godly entity who is revered by His Hindu, Muslim, Jain and Sikh followers alike as a saint, fakir, yogi and sadguru. He is believed to be an incarnation of God, who preached teachings of self-actualisation (realisation), faith, charity, compassion and patience[19].

Advaita Vedanta is one version of Vedanta, which is nominally a school of Indian philosophy, although in reality, it is a label for any hermeneutics (theory and methodology of interpretation) that attempts to provide a consistent interpretation of the philosophy of the Upanishads, or more formally, the authentic summary of the Upanishads, Badarayana's Brahma Sūtra. 'Advaita' is often translated as 'non-dualism' though it literally means 'non-secondness'. Although Adi Shankara is regarded as the promoter of Advaita Vedanta as a distinct school of Indian philosophy, the origins of this school predate Adi Shankara. The existence of an Advaita tradition is acknowledged by Adi Shankara in his commentaries. Upanishadic teachers such as Yajnavalkya, Uddalaka and Badarayaṇa, the author of the Brahma Sutra, could be considered as representing the thoughts of early Advaita.

The essential philosophy of Advaita is an idealist monism and is considered to be presented first in the Upanishads and consolidated in the Brahma Sutra by this tradition. According to Advaita metaphysics, Brahma—the ultimate, transcendent and immanent God of the latter Vedas—appears as the world because of its creative energy (maya). The world has no separate existence apart from Brahma. The experiencing self (jiva) and the transcendental self of the universe (atman) are in reality identical (both are Brahma), though the individual self seems different, just as space within a container seems different from space outside the container. These cardinal doctrines are represented in the anonymous verse, 'brahma satyam jagan mithya; jivo brahmaiva na aparah' ('Brahma is alone true, and this world of plurality is not truth; the individual self is not different from Brahma'). Plurality is experienced because of errors in judgment (mithya) and ignorance (avidya). Knowledge of Brahma removes these errors and causes liberation from the cycle of transmigration (cycle of birth, death and rebirth) and worldly bondage[20].

'Ekam sat vipra bahudha vadanti' is a sutra quote from all the Upanishads. This aphorism means, 'That which exists is One, sages called it by various names.' This idea from the Upanishads has been ingrained into the civilisation of India for thousands of years, resulting in the extreme tolerance of Hindus on the whole. Jains and Buddhists also emphasise the idea of coexistence and tolerance. This idea was further expanded in urging the masses to see God's presence in every atom of the universe, and this generated the presence of the same one soul in all living things. In the Bhagwad Gita, it was most emphatically stressed when Lord Krishna tells Arjuna that the soul is immortal and that it is fallacy to believe that you can kill anybody or anybody can kill the soul. The soul can neither be killed or kill. If the soul is one in everyone and the soul is immortal, then what was the need to fight a battle like in the Mahabharata? This is because the very same soul, when it takes the cover of the human body because of karma, also acquires good and ill qualities. Therefore, a virtuous soul–body must destroy an evil soul–body. This should be the practice of life. Life is not meant to tolerate 'ill' and become a subjugated insect-like living creature. Lack of this awareness destroys the fundamental law of the universe of 'unified "One" Energy', 'ekam Sat'[21].

Thus, 'sab ka mailk ek' is a very powerful and universally true statement made by Sai Baba. It embraces and enhances the sense of brotherhood. It transcends region, religion, caste, creed, country, language or any other such divisive element. It is a statement proclaiming universal brotherhood, just as Sai Baba never discriminated between human beings and animals. Sab ka mailk ek is the key of His teachings, and He practised and preached it throughout his life.

2. SAI SEVA

8

Cleaning Shirdi

> Within no time, Shirdi became a clean town
>
> *The irony in India is that the more popular the place of pilgrimage, the more unclean is the town where it is located. I resolved to change this perception about Shirdi. We undertook a campaign—a collaboration between the Sansthan and the local municipal council, which responded positively. Residents also participated. Within few days, Shirdi became a clean town.*

After taking charge as chairman of Shri Sai Baba Sansthan, Shirdi, I focused my attention on transforming Shirdi into a clean and green town. It became a top priority on my agenda. I put forth a proposal regarding this in the meeting of the Board of Trustees. I had met with the Hon. President of India and the Hon. Prime Minister of India when I invited them to attend Sai Baba's Samadhi Centenary Celebrations. Both were very keen on promoting public cleanliness. The then CM of Maharashtra, Hon. Shri Devendra Fadnavis, suggested that the Sansthan play a leading role and also bear the cost of the clean-up of Shirdi. So, we resolved that the Sansthan would take up the responsibility for the cleanliness of Shirdi.

We resolved to provide funds of ₹30 lakhs (₹3.0 million) per month to the municipal council for the cleanliness drive. On realising that this fund amount was insufficient, as per the instructions of the then CM Shri Devendra Fadnavis, the fund was increased to ₹42 lakhs (₹4.2 million) per month.

On the birth anniversary of Mahatma Gandhi, with the help of Sansthan employees, municipal employees, students and citizens, we decided to volunteer (shramadaan) to clean up Shirdi. When we realised that the major challenge was where to deposit the solid waste collected during the clean-up drive, the programme was postponed. There were six dried up wells where people used to dump garbage. By this time, all of them were filled to the brim. I realised that there was an urgent need to find an alternative solution. I started to look for technological solutions to this problem.

I wanted to carry out solid waste management using the latest technology. From day one, I believed that solid waste is not a burden on society but a potential source of income. I wanted to prove that if the waste is viewed from an economic, technological or business point of view, it is definitely a source of wealth.

This is a challenge for all scientists and technical experts. While approaching the issue of solid waste management, I divided the problem into four parts: 1) door-to-door collection of solid waste followed by segregation, 2) transporting it to the processing centre, 3) using the latest technology to process solid waste at the centre and lastly 4) encashing on the products generated in the process, namely the fertiliser, gas and electricity produced. Since the first two processes relate to administrative and government processes, I shall refrain from commenting on them. The third part is something that interests all technologists. But all technologists must keep in mind that a technology is useful only if it is financially viable. Otherwise, it gets reduced to a mere showpiece. LED lights are widely used these days because they are affordable even for common people. Else they would have remained decorative items. I consulted many people in this regard. Many experts were asked to make presentations on possible solutions during the meetings of the Board of Trustees. I visited solid waste processing plants at Goa, Solapur, Varanasi, Mumbai and many other cities and states. Even I studied the scenario in some countries such as Sweden.

There are different ways of processing solid waste: 1) people gather the waste into small piles and then burn it; 2) people segregate the plastic waste and use it to generate fuel; 3) the waste can be fermented using bio-organic methods to produce fertilisers and gas. The gas can be used in the kitchen or to generate electricity. While this is scientifically possible, I found that it was not sufficient. I wanted the solution to be economically viable as well. Through my study visits, I realised that sufficiently advanced technology is available, but that all problems cannot be solved alone.

For the past few years, I have been studying the issue of solid waste management. Solid waste has become a critical issue for many big cities. This problem is compounded when it comes to towns that are places of pilgrimage and attract huge crowds. We often observe that while the temples themselves are clean, the surrounding town is quite dirty. I am a nuclear scientist and have worked as Senior Scientist in the Department of Atomic Energy, Government of India, for 27 years in the field of nuclear engineering. I approached this problem from a scientific perspective.

Let us try to define solid waste: any waste can be defined as 'a left over, a redundant product or material of no or marginal value for the owner and which the owner wants to discard'[22]. And solid waste is waste in solid state. Here we are mainly talking about city or residential waste only. We are not considering here any liquid or gaseous waste or any clinical, pharmaceutical, electronic or hazardous solid waste.

A number of steps are involved in solid waste management (SWM), right from collecting, segregating, processing and disposal of waste. The first step of collecting the waste, though very important, is not discussed here as it is more administrative than scientific in nature. But the economics and corruption involved in this step can overshadow the entire process. For example, how much waste is generated in Mumbai every day? At present the figure is of 7000 tonnes. Now the question is, who measured this and how? This has no answer. It is mostly done by the contracting firms who collect and dump it in the yard. The higher the number they show, the more they earn. In the case of Mumbai, the expenses for gathering and processing solid waste are beyond imagination. One authentic source told me that the contract for collecting solid waste and transporting it to the dumping ground is worth a whopping ₹1,800 crores (₹18 billion). It is a fact that Brihanmumbai Municipal Corporation spends on tackling this issue, but the real question is what these funds are actually spent on. A major part of the expenditure is on transporting solid waste and dumping it rather than further processing it. Anyway, we are limiting ourselves to the technological part. Let us understand various technological methods available to treat the solid waste.

Technology

A number of established and alternative technologies are available to treat solid waste. Some of them are listed below[23]:

1. Autoclaving
2. Fluffing
3. Melting
4. Incineration
5. Vermicomposting
6. Energy recovery
7. Thermal conversion
8. Advanced thermal treatment
9. Plasma gasification and plasma pyrolysis
10. Refuse-derived fuel
11. Fluidised bed technology
12. Bio-conversion
13. Dry anaerobic composting

Anaerobic digestion: Researchers are working on different methods of processing solid waste. Their concepts and goals differ widely. What must be common, however, is the desire to work for the benefit of society. Mumbai generates 7000 tonnes of solid waste daily. The disposal of this waste becomes a huge challenge as a huge space is required for dumping. How long the dumping ground can be used and how to manage the piles of solid waste—all these are challenges. If technology is not used to process solid waste, the number of dumping grounds will keep increasing. Finding a solution is difficult but not impossible if technologists can apply their mind to this problem. Solid waste disposal has become a big business, and there are even garbage mafia in existence.

It is not easy to tackle the problem of solid waste disposal. However, advanced technology is available today as scientists come up with new inventions. All that is required is political and administrative willpower. I firmly believe that all the solid waste in the country can be converted into wealth. The day we accomplish this will be the day that India truly becomes Swachh Bharat. Not only will we have a cleaner environment but the expenditure on healthcare can also reduce tremendously. In addition, this solid waste can be used to generate fertilisers, gas and electricity.

Some days ago, I was reading a history of Sweden. This is the only nation in the world to process its entire solid waste output. The solid waste is used to generate different resources. *The Hindu* reported in its issue dated 12 December 2016 that Sweden ran out of garbage and had to import it from neighbouring countries. They realised that they were not getting sufficient solid waste to run their processing plants at full capacity, to produce power, they actually needed more solid waste to process. They even started to import solid waste from neighbouring countries such as Norway, Denmark and Scotland. From the technological, scientific and economic perspective, waste is nothing but wealth. Sweden has proved that waste is not a liability.

Around 20 tonnes of solid waste are generated in Shirdi daily. Around 12 to 13 tonnes of garbage are generated in the town, including that of the hotels and seven to eight tonnes by the Sansthan activities. I have resolved to set up a waste-processing plant with the capacity to process 20 tonnes of waste daily. This plant will be set up by the Sai Baba Sansthan. All the waste generated in the town and by the temple will be processed in this plant. I am confident that this project will make Shirdi truly a clean town.

All the technical formalities have been completed, and this project will be underway in the near future. This project in Shirdi will become a model project for small towns. The various technologies available are listed above. I have narrowed down to the technological method of anaerobic bio-digestion that will be used to treat the solid waste in the plant. The gas generated through this project will be used for cooking, and the fertilisers generated will be utilised for farming or gardening. We have also worked out the financial viability of the project. The project will incur an initial cost of around ₹5 crores (₹50 million). This investment can be recovered within five years through the sale of fertilisers and use of the generated gas. After five years, the project will become profitable. Seven acres of land near the helipad have been identified for the plant's location.

Anaerobic Bio-Digestion

Anaerobic bio-digestion is a series of biological processes in which microorganisms break down biodegradable material in the absence of oxygen. One of the end products is biogas, which is combusted to generate electricity and heat or can be processed into renewable natural gas and transportation fuels. A range of anaerobic digestion technologies are converting livestock manure, municipal wastewater solids, food waste, high-strength industrial wastewater and residuals, fats, oils and grease (FOG) and various other organic waste streams into biogas, 24 hours a day, seven days a week. Separated digested solids can be composted, utilised for dairy bedding, directly applied to cropland or converted into other products. Nutrients in the liquid stream are used in agriculture as fertilisers.

The Biological Process

The digestion process begins with bacterial hydrolysis of the input materials to break down insoluble organic polymers such as carbohydrates and make them available for the bacteria. Acidogenic bacteria then convert the sugars and amino acids into carbon dioxide, hydrogen, ammonia and organic acid, along with additional ammonia, hydrogen and carbon dioxide. Finally, methanogens convert these products to methane and carbon dioxide[24].

The plant is yet to be installed. Due to the Sansthan's efforts, Shirdi was ranked as the second cleanest town in

Maharashtra and the third cleanest town at the national level. Shirdi also won an award of ₹15 crores (₹150 million) from the state government, not once, but twice consecutively in 2018 and 2019. With everyone's cooperation, I was confident that Shirdi would become a clean and beautiful city. With the installation of the SWM plant, Shirdi will surely become the number one clean city in the country. I was filled with pride while felicitating the then Mayor of Shirdi Mrs Yogita Shelke (also a Trustee of the Sansthan). The felicitation was on the occasion of the Shirdi Municipal Council winning an award of ₹15 crores (₹150 million) and being ranked third in India and second in Maharashtra for cleanliness as per the Swachh Bharat campaign survey of 2018.

Shirdi is always crowded with visiting devotees, who come from all over India and from other countries as well. Though the population of the town is only around 35,000, there are about 70,000 devotees visiting Shirdi every day. Due to this, the quantity of waste generated is very large. As a result, the town generates a huge quantity of garbage. However, the cleanliness of the town has been largely neglected. I resolved to prioritise this issue. Even though the municipal council collects this waste daily, the disposal of leftover food from restaurants has been a major challenge for the municipal authorities. This food waste is now transported to the biogas plant run by the Sansthan. A waste-processing plant with the capacity of five tonnes has already been installed by the Sansthan. The Municipal Council is going to set up another such plant with equal processing capacity.

In response to Hon. PM Narendra Modi's Swachh Bharat Abhiyan, with the initiative by the municipal council, 565 toilets were constructed for private use. The Sansthan provides a fund of ₹42 lakhs (₹4.2 million) to the council every month to maintain cleanliness. The Sansthan spends crores of rupees on providing basic facilities such as roads and electricity[29].

The unique feature of the Shirdi Municipal Council activities is the active participation of the local citizens. Abhay and Yogita Shelke played a pivotal role in turning this into a movement. The clean-up movement is getting a good response from the citizens. A large number of school students participate in initiatives such as tree plantation. The NGO Green Shirdi Movement and the Shirdi Municipal Council launched a tree-plantation drive for a green Shirdi. Under this initiative, 10,000 trees have been planted in the Shirdi area, and the council has been successful in ensuring the survival of most of these trees.

A water supply project for the town has been set up at a cost of ₹37 crores (₹370 million). The water is sourced from the canal of Gangapur Dharana dam and is supplied to the homes. As a result, Shirdi no longer requires any water tankers.

In 2019, *India Today* carried out an extensive survey of all of the temple cities in India and found that Shirdi is the cleanest temple town. I received the first prize on behalf of the Sansthan at a grand function in the august presence of the Hon. President of India at New Delhi on 2 October 2019. I am satisfied to see that my vision of 'Clean Shirdi' is becoming a reality.

9

Sai Agarbatti

Two hundred local women empowered

The flowers offered to Sai Baba by devotees used to be thrown away as waste. I conceived the idea of recycling these floral offerings into incense sticks. This was an eco-friendly concept and, through the fragrance of the incense sticks, devotees would be able to delight in Baba's presence for a longer time. The resulting Agarbatti Project has given employment to 200 needy local women and has an annual turnover of ₹5 crores (₹50 million).

Devotion is a special feature of the Indian mindset. No other country can boast of such a huge population that is devoted to its deities. Sai Baba commands the devotion of crores of people, and lakhs of devotees have experienced the grace of His blessings. Devotion to Sai Baba is growing day by day.

As Sai Baba was very fond of flowers, almost every devotee offers garlands or a bunch of flowers to Baba as part of their worship. The quantity of floral offerings is very high on Thursdays, Sundays and festive days. The sheer scale of these offerings is awe-inspiring, but, on the other hand, it creates the problem of disposing of these flowers.

After becoming the chairman of the trust, I took a stroll through the temple premises. I approached Baba's samadhi through the darshan queue. Devotees were offering garlands, bouquets and flowers to Baba's idol and at the samadhi. I wondered what happened to these flowers later. I returned to my office, but this question continued to preoccupy me.

On inquiring, I learned that around two and a half tonnes of flowers are offered to Baba daily. On Thursdays, Sundays and festive days, the quantity of flowers offered goes up to three or even four tonnes. I was shocked to hear how these flowers were disposed of: they were simply thrown away as waste. It was impossible to reconcile this with my beliefs and values and really disturbed me. Since these flowers represent the feelings and devotion of the devotees, I could not wrap my head around the idea of them being thrown away as waste. Then I realised that the flowers offered to Baba could be recycled into fragrant agarbattis or incense sticks.

Before arriving at the production of agarbattis, a proposal was forcefully raised to stop floral offerings in the temple. In this process, it was revealed that hundreds of farmers from around 50 adjoining villages are involved in producing these flowers, and hundreds of people are employed in making garlands and bouquets, and hundreds of them are involved in selling them to the devotees. If the flowers were not allowed in the temple, it would make thousands of people jobless. Therefore, the suggestion was not accepted by the Sansthan and floral offerings continued as before.

I invited representatives from various organisations that produce agarbattis to discuss this issue. From among them, we selected the organisation named Eco Nirmiti Foundation. It was resolved that the Sansthan would provide floral offerings to Eco Nirmiti and that the transport arrangements for the same would be made by them. The organisation would then separate the flower petals, dry them, turn them into powder and produce agarbattis by applying glue to this powder. Eco Nirmiti started this work, and 200 local women in need of work were employed under this project. Per day, they produce 5,000 packets containing 30 agarbattis each. Each packet is sold for ₹30. This amounts to a daily income of ₹1.5 lakhs (₹0.15 million), which makes an annual turnover of around ₹5 crores (₹50 million). The Sansthan also benefits from the project, because 10 per cent of the proceeds are given to the Sansthan as per the agreement with Eco Nirmiti. Besides, the agarbattis also have emotional value for the devotees. They believe that these agarbattis carry the presence of Baba and the fragrance of devotion. As they also create wealth, these agarbattis not only carry the fragrance of devotion, they also inspire respect.

In the future, essence, dhup and gulkand could also be produced by recycling these flowers. The stems and leaves of the flowers are converted into fertiliser. In order to reach out to devotees with these agarbattis, the Sansthan has given Eco Nirmiti a room counter to sell them. These agarbattis have been received enthusiastically by devotees. They take pride in gifting them to their near and dear ones.

Earlier, due to a lack of other options, the Sansthan was forced to dump the daily floral offerings as waste at the local municipal dumping ground. We resolved to find a sustainable and long-term solution to this problem. With the cooperation of Eco Nirmiti (now Janaseva Foundation) and the involvement of women belonging to self-help groups, we set up this project of recycling the waste into agarbattis. This is a unique project that not only ensures the cleanliness of the temple premises, but also respects the feelings of devotees and infuses the entire atmosphere with devotion.

This project involves various tasks such as collecting the floral offerings from the temple, transporting them to the plant, classifying the flowers, separating the rose petals, drying them and grinding to a powder and turning them into agarbattis that give out a soft fragrance.

Ordinary enterprises are quite commonly set up. What is unique about this project is its orientation towards public service. A maximum number of women have been employed in this project. The task of collecting floral offerings from the temple has been assigned entirely to women employees. Thirty women employees work in shifts to ensure that this work is done on all seven days of the week. As women employees are more effective at canvassing the devotees about this project, which aims at cleanliness and at creating a new product, this task is given to them. The company has deployed two vehicles to transport the floral offerings to the plant.

The floral offerings to Sai Baba mostly consist of roses, zendu and sabja flowers. At present, the rose petals are used for manufacturing agarbattis, which are marketed under the name 'Sai Dwarakamai'. The other flowers are converted into a manure used for the Sansthan's gardens. But in future, agarbattis will be produced from all these flowers.

10

Blood Donation

Like hair donation at Tirupati,
blood donation at Shirdi

We worship God by offering leaves, flowers, fruits, milk and water. In appealing to devotees to donate blood, my vision was to bring about a unique blend of shraddha and service at Shirdi. Devotees visiting Tirupati for darshan donate their hair. I was confident that if we appealed to devotees at Shirdi to donate blood, it would create a massive blood donation movement. I rapidly devised a scheme and this vision became a reality.

A study by the National AIDS Control Organisation carried out in India in the year 2018 estimated a population need of 26.4 million units of blood, which implies that the country needs to collect 26.4 million units of whole blood to address the need for whole blood and its components in the country. The clinical demand in healthcare facilities across the country was estimated to be 14.6 million units of blood. According to the study, the supply was found to be 13.5 million units in 2018; however, the annual collection reported by NACO in the country was 11.1 million units in 2017. Hence, although the country might collect nearly an adequate volume of blood in terms of overall country requirement, the distribution of availability and therefore, access, may not be equitable[25].

In India, a lot of donated blood is wasted due to poor infrastructure and storage facilities. The WHO recommends that for every 1,000 people in the country, around 10 donors are needed to provide an adequate supply of blood. Thus, around 1 per cent of the population must be targeted to be voluntary blood donors. There are a lot of misconceptions about blood donation, mostly due to lack of proper education and social atmosphere. It has been reported that the myths about blood donation are a major hurdle in blood collection[26].

> I had always cherished the vision that temples and places of pilgrimage should become more socially oriented and service-oriented. I dreamed of creating a statewide blood donation campaign at Shirdi, to manifest devotion in the form of social service. With everyone's cooperation, I was able to bring this dream into reality.

Every year, India celebrates National Voluntary Blood Donation Day on 1 October to highlight the need and importance of safe blood in the life of an individual. The WHO estimates that blood donation by 1 per cent of the population is generally the minimum to meet a nation's most basic need for blood. Even by this low measure, as per data presented to the Lok Sabha on 23 March 2018, India was short of 1.9 million units of blood (or 15 per cent) vis-a-vis the WHO norm. In India, the concept of blood donation has always been demand-led, wherein even the most well-educated people perceive blood donation as an emergency service to be provided only when there is a need. Currently, most blood banks and hospitals in India are highly dependent on replacement blood donations, wherein family or friends are asked to donate blood in lieu of the units given to a patient. As a result, they are rarely able to maintain an adequate stock of different blood groups to meet the transfusion needs of all their patients, particularly in emergency situations. In addition, this puts constant pressure on patients to find blood donors in order to receive treatment.

In most aspects of healthcare, the availability of a service should precede its need. The same goes for blood. In a scenario where blood needs to be arranged to meet its need, there are risks of delays in surgical procedures, inadequate time to properly test the donor blood or effectively screen potential donors. Moreover, even some basic procedures, such as childbirth, are accompanied by risk of haemorrhage, for which an ample stock of blood is required. Even today, in many remote areas, pregnant women are forced to travel to distant hospitals to deliver their child, because the primary healthcare centres closest to them do not have sufficient blood available.

This cultural apathy of donating-as-directed coupled with widespread misinformation and ignorance about the effect, importance and safety of voluntary blood donation significantly impacts India's blood transfusion system by making it inefficient and disorganised.

Awareness needs to be increased on voluntary blood donation for this behavioural change to happen. Building a chain of voluntary blood donors who regularly donate blood allows a consistent and reliable supply of safe blood when required and becomes more cost-effective than recruiting new donors. Through voluntary blood donation, patients have improved access to safe blood transfusion as the blood and blood products they receive carry a low risk of infection that might further compromise their health.

Voluntary blood donation programmes succeed only when people are wellaware of the sense of sacrifice behind it and are motivated by altruism and the desire to help others in need as a sense of moral duty or social responsibility. Therefore, it is important that we start inculcating this mindset change in India, to build awareness and behavioural change towards voluntary blood donation.

One of the most crucial challenges that affect blood availability in India is the inadequacy of repeat voluntary blood donors. The year 2019 promised to be the year of advancement in the Indian healthcare sector with Prime Minister Modi underscoring that a healthy life is the right of every person and giving a huge thrust to accessibility and affordability of healthcare services in India[27].

Shirdi Devasthan is known across the world today. Sai devotees from all corners of the world and of India devoutly visit Shirdi for Sai Baba's darshan. It is said that 'At Shirdi, the devotion of Shegaon and the wealth of Tirupati is united'. I had always cherished the vision that temples and places of pilgrimage should become more socially oriented and service-oriented. I dreamed of creating a state-wide blood donation campaign at Shirdi, to manifest devotion in the form of social service. With cooperation from everyone, I was able to make this dream a reality.

The revered Sai Baba not only preached shraddha (faith) and saburi (patience) to his devotees, he also advocated social service. Inspired by his ideals, I proposed the initiative of blood donation—an apparently simple yet extremely crucial service to society. I was confident that once Sai devotees were made aware about the importance of blood donation and given suitable facilities for the same, they would respond to our appeal. For them, the act of blood donation would become the act of offering their most valuable possessions to Sai Baba. Thus, I introduced the innovative campaign titled 'Tirupati mein keshdan, Shirdi mein raktadan', which means 'Like hair donation at Tirupati, blood donation at Shirdi'. Devotees who visit Tirupati take great pride in donating their hair. The Sansthan appealed to Sai devotees to donate blood with the same sense of pride and sacrifice.

An average of 50,000 devotees visit Shirdi daily for Sai darshan. If we were able to convince them of the importance of blood donation, and if even 1 per cent of the visitors donated blood, we would still collect 500 units of blood every day.

The Sansthan put up banners appealing for blood donation in the temple premises. A blood collection facility was set up in the temple premises, and this was the beginning of a mahayagna—a mega campaign of blood donation. Initially, the response was small, but it started growing. Later, it reached a point where we were forced to say, 'Please do not donate blood as our capacity for storage is exhausted.' In the trustee meeting, we came up with a solution for this problem. We decided to tie up with the blood banks of government institutions and NGOs. Initially, we appealed to a few blood banks to collect blood from Shirdi. Eventually, around 25 blood banks became associated with this blood donation campaign. At present, an average of 150–200 persons donate blood daily. In the samadhi centenary year of Sai Baba, the Sansthan collected around 50,000 units of blood. Though this is highly creditable, it does not constitute even 1 per cent of the devotees. The number can be increased so as to collect 500 units of blood daily. That is the ultimate target.

In the year 2000, a blood bank was set up at Shirdi. Rather than making devotees come to the blood bank, we wanted the blood bank to reach the devotees. So the blood donation facility was set up in the temple premises itself. In 2004, a well-equipped centre for collecting blood was started. The then Chief Minister Vilasrao Deshmukh inaugurated this campaign. Initially, blood donation facilities were available on two days in the week. At present, blood is collected on all seven days of the week. We decided to inscribe this in the minds of the devotees: just as you come to Shirdi for darshan of Sai Baba, you must also donate blood. The donors are awarded with a certificate and honoured with a direct darshan of Sai Baba. This has helped promote the blood donation campaign and has boosted the enthusiasm of blood donors.

There are more than 8,000 Sai temples all over India and around 450 Sai temples in other countries. We have suggested to all that this blood donation movement should be run at all these temples. Thursday is an especially sacred day for Sai Baba, so I have appealed to Sai devotees to donate blood on Thursday.

I believe that blood donation by devotees during the centenary year celebrations was a significant public service. The success of this project convinced me that it must have been blessed by Sai Baba Himself. I hope that the story of this initiative will provide inspiration to many institutions.

If service is imbued with devotion, it reaches the feet of the Almighty. From this thought was born my idea of appealing to the devotees visiting Shirdi to donate blood. In a short time, this idea became a mega campaign.

The blood donated by Sai devotees is provided free of cost to the patients at Sainath Hospital. It is also provided free of cost to patients of Sai Baba Hospital admitted under the Mahatma Phule Scheme.

During the Sai Baba Samadhi Centenary Year, the Sansthan organised a mega blood donation camp. It was held on 30 December 2017, and more than 1,000 units of blood were collected in this camp. Around 22 blood banks participated in this initiative.

The blood donation movement is very well managed by Dr Maithili Pitambare of Sainath Hospital.

The blood bank at the Sansthan has the advanced equipment required to carry out the analysis and component separation of the blood we collect. One unit of blood benefits three patients. Dr Suryakant Patil ably manages this department with his team of 24 colleagues. In 2017, the blood bank collected 16,000 units of blood. We are rapidly advancing towards making Sai Sansthan the largest blood donation centre in the entire state. I am sure that this seed of blood donation will spread to all the Sai temples and it will become a national movement of blood donation.

If each of us understands the importance of blood donation and the saying 'Blood donor of today may be a blood receiver tomorrow', we shall never face a shortage of blood. The Sansthan is thus making comprehensive efforts to fulfil its social responsibility. The lion's share of the credit for the successful campaign goes to the employees of the blood bank. It is always energising to meet them.

It may be noted that there is no alternative to human blood. Efforts to create artificial blood by scientists have not been fully successful, though partial success has been achieved. The blood so created cannot perform all the functions of natural blood, but it can do so to a limited extent[28].

Keshdan in Tirupati, raktadan in Shirdi.

11

Dava Aur Dua

Sai Baba placed great emphasis on medical care

He cured many patients and freed them from the clutches of disease. Inspired by His example, two well-equipped hospitals with 575 beds, including a super specialty hospital, have been functioning in his memory at Shirdi for a number of years. There was a constant shortage of medicines. Medicines worth ₹66 crore were purchased to mitigate this shortage. Many of the machines at the hospital were over 15 years old. As many as 128 new machines, including Cath Lab, CT Scan and MRI machines were newly purchased at a cost of ₹35 crore (₹350 million). A number of medical camps were held. We attempted to make them ultra-modern hospitals. Shri Sainath Hospital was made entirely free of cost starting from 1 January 2017. This is a small attempt to make readers aware of the existing medical facilities at Shirdi and our attempts to modernise them.

Many theories float around the globe. Often, the proponents of these theories are themselves not serious about their practical application. A theory cannot be established unless it is proven that it can be put into practice. Theory alone is a dry entity; unless it is put into practice, it has little or no value. At Shri Sai Baba Sansthan, Shirdi, you can find actual examples of Sai's philosophy being implemented in the real world. Now that we are conversant with the Sai philosophy, we also need to know its practical application. I have thrown light on this crucial aspect of Shri Sai Baba Sansthan, Shirdi, in this and the following chapters. This chapter gives an overview of the healthcare provided at Shirdi.

Feeding the hungry and serving patients were close to Baba's heart. The essence of His life was service. In addition to the mantra of shraddha (faith) and saburi (patience), Sai Baba advocated service, with a special emphasis on service of the sick and ailing. He would lovingly care for patients. Even today, the eyes of Sai Baba idols or paintings manifest his compassion and maternal love. One loving glance from His eyes would suffice to relieve the pain of suffering devotees[29].

On reading *Shri Sai Satcharitra*—the story of Sai Baba's life—one learns about various incidents that reflect His deep concern for patients. It is through Sai Baba's inspiration that Shirdi Sansthan now manages two hospitals at Shirdi. These hospitals are performing sterling service towards society.

Having access to well-equipped modern hospitals in a small town like Shirdi seems impossible. But the Sai Sansthan has successfully completed this task. A huge number of devotees visit Shirdi for darshan. The Sansthan has set up two hospitals for the benefit of the devotees as well as the residents of Shirdi and the country. Free or low-cost treatment, prompt service and compassion towards patients are the hallmarks of these hospitals.

I surveyed these hospitals and observed that they were equipped to offer excellent service and proper facilities. However, awareness about the medical facilities in Shirdi among the people was very low. Various efforts would have to be taken to create this awareness. Along with it, we needed to further modernise the hospitals and equip them more fully. The latest equipment and ultra-modern machines for treatment were required. I decided to make this a priority by finding ways to purchase these machines. I also prepared a detailed plan for conducting various medical camps in order to make the common people aware of the medical facilities available. I attempted to publicise the medical camps among the poor and needy through extensive use of mass/social media. This could be accomplished through the different programmes that would be organised during the Sai Samadhi Centenary celebrations.

A record number of patients benefited from these camps. Another significant achievement was the Sainath Hospital at Shirdi, which started offering free-of-cost treatment from 1 January 2017 and is one of its kind in India.

The two hospitals managed by the Sansthan have proudly kept the flag of medical service flying. They are renowned not only in the state of Maharashtra but in the entire country. Patients from various parts of India come to these hospitals for treatment. Sainath Hospital (with 325 beds) and Sai Baba Super Speciality Hospital (with 250 beds) treat around 5.5 lakh (0.55 million) patients every year. Sometimes, patients who were refused admission or were asked to give up hope by renowned hospitals elsewhere have come to Shirdi and have been miraculously cured. By the medical treatment by the skilled doctors and the blessings of Sai Baba combined, the percentage of patients who recover is very high.

Sainath Hospital had a humble beginning as a dispensary in 1964. Today, it is a well-equipped hospital with 325 beds. General surgery, general medicine, paediatrics, gynaecology, orthopaedics, ENT, ophthalmology, dentistry, physiotherapy—all these treatments are offered here. Besides allopathy, homeopathic and Ayurvedic treatments are also provided. The healing touch that is full of care and compassion is a unique feature of the treatment carried out here. The doctors have introduced a number of innovative initiatives that have benefited thousands of patients. Internationally renowned doctors from all over the world specially participate in these initiatives.

The mobile clinic and the first aid centre at the Sai Mandir are seemingly simple services, but they have benefited a large number of patients. The mobile clinic consists of a well-equipped ambulance from the hospital that caters to around five to seven villages outside Shirdi. Every ambulance is equipped with a team containing one doctor, one pharmacist, one staff nurse and one medical attendant. The ambulance halts at a predetermined place in every village. Patients from the village gather there, they are examined and given medicines there itself, which are free of cost. Villagers who tend to ignore minor ailments and women who cannot find the time for medical treatment due to the burden of work are the main beneficiaries of this scheme.

The First Aid Centre in the temple area is another apparently simple but very useful scheme. There are two such centres near the temple, and they offer their services from 6 am to 11 pm every day. On festive days or heavily crowded days, first aid is offered at six locations, including Bhakta Niwas and Prasadalaya (mess). The First Aid Centres offer primary treatment to the devotees visiting Shirdi for darshan. The hospital administration has identified the needs of the devotees and found a creative way to fulfil them.

The General Surgery department of the hospital has won special renown. It is staffed by skilled doctors such as Dr Ram Naik. He works unceasingly from 8 in the morning to 10 at night and has successfully performed complicated surgeries such as pancreatic surgery. Dr Ramdas Awhad has been working in the Ayurvedic department for the past 18 years without accepting remuneration of any kind. In the ophthalmology department, 20 to 25 cataract surgeries are performed daily using the new phaco method.

The Sainath Hospital has an intensive care unit (ICU) with eight beds. From 1 January 2017, all the treatments at this hospital have been offered free of cost. The patient is only required to pay ₹10 for the initial case paper. This was a historic decision. Many patients from all over the country come to the hospital for treatment. Not only are the patients given free food, but their relatives are also given free of cost meals from the Prasadalaya. Residential arrangements for the patients' relatives are also made free of cost. The relatives are provided free transport in buses that ply between the hospitals and the residential buildings.

A government centre for treatment of TB and AIDS has been set up in the hospital. The Sansthan has provided the space required for this centre.

There are specific guidelines, following which poor and needy patients are given a grant of ₹25,000/-. This amount is handed over to the hospital where the patient goes for further treatment. This scheme has been running since 1964. The scheme has now been revised to increase the grant to ₹50,000/-.

At present, 64 doctors are working at the hospital. There are eight visiting doctors. If we include the doctors who volunteer on special occasions, the number of doctors is around 100.

Skilled doctors, free-of-cost treatment and the compassionate care given by the hospital staff—these factors attract a large number of patients to these hospitals. The patients come not only from Maharashtra but from all parts of the nation. Devotion towards Sai Baba also brings patients for treatment.

Seven Special Medical Camps

An innovative project that we implemented was the organisation of special medical camps for various diseases during the Sai Samadhi Centenary celebrations. Seven special medical camps were organised during this year with very good response. One of the purposes of these camps was to spread awareness in the villages about the medical facilities in Shirdi.

The first medical camp was for an eye check-up. Thousand patients were examined and given suitable spectacles. If suitable spectacles were not readily available for some patients, they were prepared and delivered to them after the camp. Mr Prakash Gangavani gave special assistance for organising this camp. Dr Saumil Kothari from Vision Eye Foundation, Mumbai, participated in the camp for cataract treatment. In two days, he and his team of colleagues performed 107 surgeries to remove cataracts and correct strabismus.

In January 2018, a medical camp for the treatment of kidney stones was conducted. Dr Ketan Shukla from Ahmedabad is a nationally renowned expert in this kind of surgery. He visits Shirdi hospital four to five times a year, bringing with him his own well-equipped medical van. He has successfully performed even the most complicated surgeries.

The Jaipur Foot Camp (prosthetic leg) held in February can be called the crowning glory of our efforts. The Mumbai branch of Bhagwan Mahavir Vikalang Sahayata Samiti provided special assistance in organising it. During this six-day camp, 709 patients received treatment. Dr D.R. Mehta, who has been honoured with Padma Bhushan and is the former Chairman of SEBI, travelled from Jaipur to visit the camp. The 85-year-old Dr Mehta personally spoke to every single patient who received treatment on the day of his visit. Not a single patient who participated in the camp was sent away without treatment. Some years ago, Dr Mehta was the victim of an accident in which he injured his leg. He was confined to bed for many days. He was distressed by imagining the plight of those who lost their legs due to accidents. This distress led him to invent the Jaipur Foot, a prosthetic foot. Along with the Jaipur Foot Camp, a camp for prosthetic arms was also held. The Rotary Club of Pune Downtown gave special assistance for this camp, in which 74 patients were fitted with prosthetic arms.

Plastic surgery can be considered one of the miracles in the field of medicine. A plastic surgery camp was conducted under the leadership of the well-known surgeon Dr Ram Chilgar on behalf of the Aurangabad branch of the FIE Foundation. Nine expert doctors from countries such as Taiwan, Singapore, Philippines, Peru and the USA visited Shirdi to participate in this camp. The world-renowned plastic surgeon from Taiwan, Dr Hung Chi-Chen supervised the conduct of the camp. The 70-year-old Dr Chen has developed a surgery for elephantiasis. He himself operated on a patient of elephantiasis in the camp. In the same camp, a very difficult operation on veins was successfully performed. Skin transplants were carried out for victims of burns. A total of 88 surgeries were performed during the three days of the camp, all free of cost. An ENT surgery and hearing aid distribution camp as well as a kidney stone treatment camp were held.

Modern Departments and Skilled Doctors

The hospitals are equipped with the departments of cardiology, neurology, cardiac surgery, neurosurgery, orthopaedics, maxillofacial surgery, general medicine, general surgery, anaesthesiology, spine and joint, radiology, dental, paediatric surgery, oncosurgery, urology, plastic surgery, gastroenterology, dietetics, physiotherapy and chest physicians.

Sai Baba Super Specialty Hospital

In accordance with Sai Baba's teachings that the service to patients is service to God, the Sai Baba Super Specialty Hospital was set up by the Sansthan in 2006. The hospital has 250 beds, and a large number of patients from Maharashtra as well as from other states are treated here.

Over the last 14 years, the hospital has acquired a highly positive reputation. I cherished the dream of making it a leading hospital in India by modernising it with the latest medical equipment and treatments. Whenever I went to Shirdi, visiting both the hospitals and conversing with the patients was a part of my routine. I would talk to the patients with concern and learn first-hand about their problems and difficulties. This knowledge helped me identify what steps could be taken to improve the facilities offered by the hospitals. One of the thrust areas I identified was the replacement of all the old machines with the latest ones of higher capacity. I got special grants sanctioned by the Board of Trustees of the Sansthan and the Government of Maharashtra for the purchase of specific machines. The purchase of foreign-manufactured machines was carried out as follows: CT scan: ₹6.74 crores (₹67.4 million); MRI: ₹15.60 crores (₹156 million), cath lab: ₹5.06 crores (₹50.6 million) and 2D Echo: ₹0.73 crores (₹7.3 million). Within a short period of time, Shri Sai

Baba Super Specialty Hospital has become renowned for the super-specialised treatment of heart diseases, brain diseases, diseases of the spine, kidney diseases, joint replacement, etc., not only in the state, but all over India. Dr Vijay Narode played a key role in the modernisation of the hospital.

A majority of patients come from the districts surrounding Shirdi, while some patients come from other parts of the country, having heard of the reputation of the hospitals. Some notable cases are the successful heart surgeries performed on the four-year-old Kavya Ghule from Ambegaon, Pune District, and on the two-and-half-year-old Rudrambh Patil from Muktainagar near Jalgaon. On an average, five to six heart surgeries are performed daily at the hospital.

Rates for Medical Tests and Treatment

The rates for treatment at Shri Sai Baba Hospital have been determined keeping in mind the poor and needy patients. The treatments here cost 30–40 per cent less than those at other hospitals. The most important aspect is that not a single patient is given poor treatment unlike what happens in many hospitals, just to extract money.

Mahatma Phule Jan Arogya Yojana (Mahatma Phule Health Care Scheme)

At present, the Maharashtra Government's ambitious scheme—Mahatma Phule Jan Arogya Yojana (earlier known as Rajiv Gandhi Jeevandayee Jan Arogya Yojana)—is being implemented at Shri Sai Baba Hospital. Recently Ayushman Bharat Yojana has also been implemented, under which patients from all over the nation can receive super-specialty treatment free of cost. Under this scheme, thousands of patients have received the benefit of free surgeries for different heart conditions.

The new scheme offers greater ease of access compared to the previous scheme. Applications under the scheme get approved within just two or three hours. As per the regulations governing the scheme, tests, surgery and treatment are conducted free of cost. Also, at the time of discharge, the patient is given sufficient medicines for 10 days and the fare to travel back to their native village in cash. The majority of the patients and their families are satisfied with the treatment under this scheme. Overall, the Mahatma Phule Jan Arogya Yojana is a blessing for patients and their families. It is also easy for the hospital management to implement. As a special grant, this scheme has been implemented by the Maharashtra state government at Shri Sai Baba Hospital, which is registered as a 'Referring Hospital'. Once a patient is registered under this scheme, they receive free-of-cost treatment, right from making the case paper up to the surgery. Under this scheme, 43,993 outpatients have been treated free of cost till date. Similarly, 18,414 patients were admitted to the hospital for free-of-cost treatment.

According to a survey conducted by the Maharashtra state government under this scheme, the Shri Sai Baba Hospital is ranked first in Maharashtra for cardiology and cardiac surgery. Shri Sai Baba Hospital has treated 9,646 cases of cardiology and 8,979 cases of cardiac surgery and received grants of around ₹13 crores (₹130 million) till date.

Free-of-cost Dialysis

Shri Sai Baba Hospital offers dialysis using the latest machines for the benefit of kidney patients. Till date, dialysis has been performed on approximately 24,628 patients. This dialysis facility has been offered completely free of cost at Shri Sai Baba Hospital from 1 January 2017. Five dialysis machines are currently operational and around 15 to 20 patients undergo dialysis every day. A separate dialysis machine is made available for jaundice patients.

Cath Lab Department

In 2006, the catheterisation lab department was set up at Shri Sai Baba Hospital for treating patients with heart conditions. Till date, the cath lab has performed procedures on 67,380 patients. The cath lab machine, which was in use for 15 years, has been replaced with an ultra-modern one. It is manufactured by Shimadzu Corporation, Japan, and around 250 tests were conducted before the machine was installed in the hospital. New MRI and CT scan machines were also purchased for the hospital. To bring the technology up to the latest standards, 128 machines at the hospital were replaced with newer models. The previous machines were more than 15 years old and in some cases, their depreciated value had dropped even below the maintenance costs. The decision to replace all the machines with new, latest models was a very revolutionary one. With the support from the trustees, I was able to successfully implement this decision.

PM National Relief Fund (Pant Pradhan Rashtriya Sahayata Nidhi)

Shri Sai Baba Hospital has been registered under the PM National Relief Fund by the central government. The registration was carried out at the recommendation by the Ministry of Health and Family Welfare. The Sai Baba Hospital was recommended because it offers proper medical facilities, highly qualified and skilled doctors and paramedical, nursing and administrative staff, the latest technology, low-cost treatment and various facilities to patients.

Special Free-of-cost Medical Treatment

With the approval of the managing committee, Shri Sai Baba Sansthan offers free-of-cost treatment to its permanent employees. Contractual employees can also avail this benefit based on their years of service. Free-of-cost medical treatment is provided to the students on the educational campuses of the Sansthan and the residents of Shri Dwarkamai Old Age Home, Upasani

Maharaj Kanya Kumari Ashram, Mahanubhav Ashram and Samvatsar. Victims of dog and snake bites are given injections free of cost, and patients of haemophilia from Ahmednagar district also receive free injections. Free-of-cost medical treatment is provided as required to the devotees who visit Shirdi for darshan.

Free Diagnostic Camps

Free diagnostic camps are conducted in remote villages of Maharashtra that do not have access to medical facilities. Patients who require surgery or further treatment are identified and invited to Shirdi.

Waivers in Medical Bill Payments

Under the Bombay Public Trust Act 1950 and the provisions of the scheme as per the High Court, 10 per cent of patients below the poverty line shall be treated free of cost at hospitals. A monthly report of the same is submitted to the Charity Commissioner, Maharashtra State, Mumbai, and the Assistant Charity Commissioner, Ahmednagar. This department also provides guidance to the patients and their families from time to time.

Honouring the Girl Child

One touching initiative by the hospital needs to be specially highlighted. Around 50 women deliver babies at the hospital every month. Mr Rajendra Kote, Chairman of Shiladhi Pratishthan, and Mr Tushar Shelke, Vice Chairman, started a unique initiative to promote the 'Save the Girl Child' movement. Every girl child born in the hospital during the centenary year was honoured with the gift of a silver coin. Every mother who gave birth to a girl child would be felicitated in a touching ceremony attended by the doctors and nurses. This unique expression of care and concern stands testimony to the social responsibility and respect for women shown by Shiladhi Pratishthan and the hospital staff.

A very touching advertisement about thalassemia used to be shown on television. It features a young girl suffering from thalassemia. She thanks most of the people she meets. On being asked why, she replies, 'I am a patient of thalassemia. I need to undergo blood transfusions very often. I think that you might be someone who donated blood to me. So, I thank everyone.' On hearing this, a touched and somewhat baffled man replies, 'But child, I have never donated blood to you.' The girl replies, 'That's ok. Maybe you haven't, but you can keep my thanks for when you donate blood in future. Well, I must go and thank many others now.' This advertisement had a strong emotional impact on me. I sincerely felt that the hospitals at Shirdi should give treatment for thalassemia too. I discussed it with the hospital authorities. They took planned efforts and hospitals started giving treatment for this incurable disease.

Thalassemia is a genetic disorder. Due to it, the creation of haemoglobin in the body slows down.

The symptoms of this disease manifest within three months. The amount of blood in the body of the patient is reduced and the patient requires frequent blood transfusions. As per the WHO, around 7,000–10,000 babies born in India every year suffer from thalassemia. At present, around ten lakh babies in India are affected by thalassemia. Such patients are given free blood transfusions by the Shri Sainath Blood Bank.

Record Number of Cardiac Surgeries

Shri Sai Baba had a special concern for the sick and ailing. The Shri Sai Baba Hospital was started in order to carry forward Sai Baba's teachings of service to patients and the hospital has progressed rapidly. In the year 2007, a total of 1,300 cardiac surgeries were performed at the hospital. A special mention must be made of the 47 cardiac surgeries performed in the 24 hours from 24 February 2007 to 25 February 2007. These 47 surgeries set a new world record. The surgeries were performed under the leadership of Dr Aniruddha Dharmadhikari. This achievement was recorded in the Guinness Book and the Limca Book of World Records.

The percentage cure rate of patients is very high due to the dava of the doctors and the dua of Shri Sai Baba. Such a good healthcare facility in the remote place of Shirdi is the pride of the town.

12

Sai Sevak

Sai Sevak: A unique manifestation of devotion

Even after I took charge as the chairman, the experience in the darshan queue kept nagging in my mind. I had returned without taking darshan, feeling humiliated. I started my duties with the memory of the humiliation fresh in my mind. I resolved to tackle the inconvenience faced by the thousands of devotees visiting Shirdi daily. My service to Sai would be meaningful if I completed even this one task.

We have a tradition of seeing God in the form of His devotees. When we bow down to a warkari (one who walks from home to Pandharpur and back) who has returned from Pandharpur, we gain the satisfaction of having bowed down to Vitthal himself. Gadge Maharaj went to Pandharpur a number of times and constructed a dharmashala (free accommodation) and a ghaat (wharf) for devotees. But he never entered the temple. He believed that service to devotees is the best worship of the Lord. I decided to implement an innovative concept—the Sai Sevak Scheme—where devotees take care of other devotees, so that the devotees visiting Shirdi receive proper facilities and hassle-free darshan.

Apace with the rapid progress of science and technology in India, faith in God is growing. As a result, places of worship have record numbers of visiting devotees on festive occasions and even on ordinary days. Vaishnodevi, Tirupati, Padmanabh Mandir, Rameshwar, Madurai, Mantralaya, Dharmasthal, Siddhivinayak Mandir, Shani Shingnapur, Gajanan Maharaj Mandir, Shegaon and other temples are witnessing this phenomenon. Shirdi, which is a beloved destination of people not only in India but all over the world, attracts a growing number of devotees. An average of 50,000–70,000 devotees per day visit the Shirdi Sai Mandir for darshan. On many days of the month, the number crosses one lakh. On festive days such as Ram Navami, Guru Poornima or Dussehra, the number of visiting devotees exceeds three lakhs. The trustees and the administration of Shirdi Sansthan strive continuously to ensure that all the devotees receive proper darshan of their God. Lodging and meals also need to be provided for devotees coming from far-off places.

The Sansthan chalked out an innovative scheme named Sai Sevak to implement crowd management and control, maintain discipline and ensure the comfort of devotees. Very soon, the Sai Sevak Scheme became a special feature of the Sansthan.

Being a scientist, I always insist that every task must be done with discipline and precision. Rather than bringing in outsiders to manage the darshan crowd and to provide various facilities, I wanted to accomplish it through self-motivated devotee participation.

I was aware that an innovative system of service by volunteers was run at Gajanan Maharaj Mandir, Shegaon. I visited Shegaon myself to learn about this system. Shiv Shankar Bhau Patil, Chairman of the Gajanan Maharaj Mandir Sansthan, helped me understand the working of this system. Shiv Shankar Bhau had some reservations about whether a similar system would work in Shirdi, but I was determined. I told him to give me his blessings and I would do it successfully. We decided to implement this system, and the devotees gave us an overwhelming response.

The number of devotees visiting Shirdi is very large when compared to those visiting Shegaon. Managing the diverse crowd from across India and 43 other countries and providing them with various facilities in an organised manner is a huge challenge. The volunteers under the Sai Sevak Scheme of the Sansthan devotedly fulfil these responsibilities.

The Sai Sevak Scheme was launched on Guru Purnima, 29 July 2017. The scheme has been functioning continuously and with undiminished enthusiasm ever since. Volunteer devotees take up duties at the darshan queue, Prasadalay, sale of Prasad ladoos, security, restaurant, bhakta-niwas and the hospital. These volunteers are called Sai Sevaks.

The scheme has been meticulously planned to run uninterrupted all year round. Ten groups of 21 volunteers each are selected for service for every week. So, a total of 210 Sai Sevaks work throughout the week. The week of service begins on Tuesday and concludes on the following Monday. The volunteers work in shifts from 6 am to 2 pm and from 2 pm to 10 pm. They go about their duties joyfully, chanting 'Om Sai Ram'. Palkhi mandals—those who carry Sai Baba's palanquin every year on their shoulders to Shirdi—have been permitted to register more than one group of volunteers per week, and groups are allowed to perform service for more than one week, if they so desire. The members of various palkhi mandals are given priority as Sai Sevaks because they have an understanding of hardship, which they experience during their Palkhi Yatra. Members of such mandals can create a group of at least 21 volunteers and register themselves with the Sansthan. With 10 groups every week, we wanted 520 groups to register to cover the year. But the response to the scheme was so overwhelming that on the very first day 570 groups got registered, thus making it a full house on the very first day.

The Sai Sevaks in every group are allotted specific duties. They happily undertake the service, whether it is applying gandha to devotees' foreheads, serving water, distributing prasad, serving meals, giving information at stalls or helping patients at the hospital.

The Sansthan provides certain facilities for the Sai Sevaks to be able to work efficiently. The Sevaks are issued with an identity card by the Sansthan and are given a uniform to be worn during volunteer service. They are provided free-of-cost accommodation, breakfast and meals by the Sansthan. If a Sai Sevak falls ill during the volunteer service, they are given free treatment at the Sansthan hospitals.

At the same time, the Sansthan has also defined certain rules for Sai Sevaks. Mr Suryabhan Game played a key role in the design and implementation of this system. Any volunteer who breaks these rules or misbehaves in any way is immediately relieved from their volunteer duties. The Sai Sevaks can work only in the allotted departments and are not allowed to select the kind of duty they want to perform. The system is so well organised that by rotation everyone gets to serve in various places, including one day in the Samadhi Mandir. On completing their week of volunteer work, the Sevaks must return their uniform, service card and identity card to the Sansthan. The rules also state that a police complaint will be registered against any Sai Sevak found to be committing fraud or promoting superstition.

At first, police verification was made mandatory before registering a Sai Sevak. While this rule has been relaxed, however, an affidavit from the chief of the concerned palkhi mandal is required.

The Sai Sevak Scheme received an overwhelming response, since every devotee yearns to serve Sai. It created a record of sorts. The remarkable feature is that these volunteers do not get remuneration in any form, except for free-of-cost lodging and board. The largest number of Sai Sevaks come from Andhra Pradesh. As many as 250 groups containing 5,300 volunteers from Andhra have rendered service to Sai. Maharashtra ranks second, with 188 groups containing 3,619 volunteers. Groups of Sai Sevaks have come from West Bengal, Tamil Nadu, Kerala and Uttarakhand as well. Some groups of volunteers have even travelled from other countries such as Malaysia, Dubai and Oman.

The devotees coming for darshan being asked to manage the other devotees is a fine example of community participation. I appealed to the devotees: just as we see Lord Vitthal in a warkari from Pandharpur, we can serve Sai in the form of devotees coming for Sai darshan.

Sai Sevaks need to have moral rules to govern their conduct. We formulated an oath which is to be sworn by every Sai Sevak before commencing their duties. The oath is as follows:

I hereby swear that…

I (name) swear in the name of Shri Sai Baba that, as a Sai Sevak—

- *I shall always practise cleanliness*
- *I shall always refrain from any addiction*
- *I shall not indulge in any misbehaviour*
- *I shall always strive to eradicate superstition*
- *I shall always follow Shri Sai Baba's mantra of shraddha and saburi*
- *I shall serve everyone with complete devotion*
- *I shall behave humbly and politely with everyone*
- *I shall uphold the respect of the post of Sai Sevak with mind, body and speech.*

Om Sai Ram!

At the inauguration of the Sai Sevak Scheme, I expressed the thought behind the concept. I told the volunteers, 'The post you will occupy is a unique one. You have not attained it through any form of competition. You must bear in mind that by selecting you for service, Baba has given you a huge opportunity. You have been selected because of Baba's love for you. The seven days you spend here will be only a starting point of your service. You have willingly accepted the mantle of service and should humbly bear it throughout your lives. The concept of Sai Sevak carries special meaning. There are many employees who work at the Sansthan, but you are Sevaks. There is a distinction between work and service, just as there is a difference between water and teertha. Scientifically, both are water and can be represented as H_2O. However, they differ in their significance. When water is imbued with devotion, it becomes teertha. Similarly, when work is performed with devotion, it becomes service.'

Unique feature of the Sai Sevak Scheme

Another unique feature of the Sai Sevak Scheme is the accidental insurance scheme coverage provided. The Sansthan obtains an accidental insurance cover of one lakh rupees for every volunteer who completes one week of service as a Sai Sevak. This facility was started from 17 July 2018, and Sai Sevaks have been awarded the insurance certificates.

Every service matters, irrespective of how small the task may be. Teertha is consumed in a small spoonful—no one asks for a glass full of teertha. But that small spoonful of teertha is sufficient to purify the full body and mind. The same goes for service. A small amount of service can achieve what remains unattainable through tonnes of work. You must perform your service with this devoted mindset.

Certificate in appreciation of service

The Sansthan implemented a number of innovative concepts under the Sai Sevak Scheme. A common ceremony is held to welcome the new groups of volunteers and to bid farewell to the groups who have completed their service. The volunteers who have completed service share their experiences and the senior employees of the Sansthan provide guidance to the new volunteers. Certificates of completion of service are awarded, and the new volunteers are administered the oath.

13

Mega Kitchen

Prasadalaya—serving food as the blessings of Sai Baba

Cooking meals for 70,000 to 100,000 people every day is a massive challenge. At Shirdi Prasadalaya, which has been serving devotees for a number of years now, this task is accomplished with ease. The grace of Sai is evident from the fact that not a single devotee leaves the Prasadalaya without a meal. The prasad is offered entirely free of cost from 1 January 2017. A new automated machine that can make 25,000 chapatis per hour has been installed. Telecast on National Geographic channel, this mega kitchen runs on solar energy. A brief overview of the project is given here.

When I visited the Prasadalaya, I was astounded by the sheer scale of the work that happens there daily. The Prasadalaya is the kitchen where meals for 50,000–70,000 devotees are cooked and served daily. On festive days, the number of meals cooked rises to one lakh. Since food is prepared on a huge scale, there are possibilities of error and food wastage. Cooking and serving food is a laborious task.

Sai Darshan by Hon. President of India Shri Ramnath Kovind with his family

Group photo with the trustees

Honouring President Kovind in Delhi:
Suresh Haware and Nalini Haware

Shirdi International Airport inauguration

Felicitating the Hon. President of India

Sai Darshan by Hon. Prime Minister Shri Narendra Modi

Welcoming Hon. Prime Minister Shri Narendra Modi at Sai Temple, Shirdi

Group photo of the trustees with Hon. Prime Minister Shri Narendra Modi

Honouring Hon. PM Shri Narendra Modi inside the Sai Temple, Shirdi

Felicitating Hon. Vice President of India Shri Venkaiah Naidu in Shirdi

Shatabdi Dhwaj Stambh at Shirdi

Welcoming Hon. Venkaiah Naidu

Felicitating Hon. Venkaiah Naidu

Felicitating the then CM Hon. Shri Devendra Fadnavis

Receiving the then CM Hon. Shri Devendra Fadnavis

Sai Darshan by Sarsanghchalak (Chief) of the RSS Dr Mohan Bhagwat

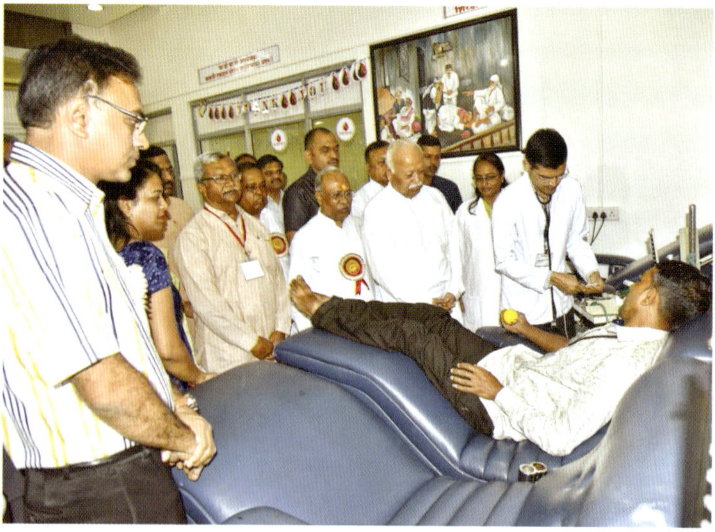

Dr Mohan ji Bhagwat at the Blood Donation Centre in Shirdi Temple

Felicitating Hon. Dr Mohan ji Bhagwat in Sai Samadhi Mandir

Hon. Union Home Minister Shri Amit Shah taking Sai Paduka Darshan

Welcoming Hon. Ch. Vidyasagar Rao

Honouring Hon. Shri Nitin Gadkari

Honouring the late Shri Manohar Parrikar

Honouring Hon. Shivraj Singh Chauhan, CM of MP

In conversation with Yoga Guru Shri Baba Ramdev

Guru Sthan and the neem tree at Shirdi

Shri Sai Baba Super Specialty Hospital at Shirdi

Prosthetic Leg (Jaipur Foot) and Hand Camp at Shirdi

Visiting and enquiring about patients at Sainath Hospital, Shirdi

Sai Baba Himself nursing a patient

Participants of the Global Sai Temple Summit at Shirdi

Neem trees grown by tissue culture at Guru Sthan

I was struck by the thought that the latest machines could be harnessed to lighten some of the workload. I decided to bring in machines to make chapatis, chop vegetables and wash the plates and bowls. The newly procured chapati-making machine makes 25,000 chapatis every hour. When your vision is progressive, its impact is assuredly positive.

I observed that a huge amount of food was being wasted daily at the Prasadalaya. Through a proper survey, I learned that the daily food wastage amounted to around five tonnes. After detailed study, I came up with certain solutions to address the issues. I found that the servers in the Prasadalaya were serving large helpings to each devotee to minimise the number of times they had to walk among the tables. This led the devotees to waste food because they could not finish all the food served. Trolleys were being used to carry the food to the tables, but the wheels of the trolleys malfunctioned. So, the servers were stationing the trolley at one point and serving food from there to the tables, which resulted in a lot of spillage. The floor tiles in the Prasadalaya were cracked, thereby obstructing and damaging the trolley wheels. I had the wheels of all the trolleys replaced with ball bearings and got the floor tiles replaced with sturdy 65 mm granite flooring. Now, the trolleys can be wheeled around smoothly. I replaced the big serving spoons and ladles with smaller ones. The size of the bowls meant for serving dal and vegetables was also reduced.

Wastage was also caused because the food items were excessively spicy. It was decided that the food would be made less spicy and that green chillies would be served to those who requested spicier food. Sai Sevaks with plaques that stated 'This food is prasad. Please do not waste it' were deputed to walk among the tables. They started requesting devotees to not leave food on their plates. As a cumulative effect of these measures, the food wastage was reduced from 5 tonnes to just 0.75 tonnes per day, a whopping 85 per cent reduction in the wastage. This means that the food wastage per head reduced to only 19 g. Employees are striving towards zero food wastage. The person in charge of the Prasadalaya, Shri Vishnu Thorat, is a wonderful person who has taken a keen interest in reducing the food wastage. A significant quantity of food is being saved from wastage every day.

Trustees of the Sai Baba Sansthan have also introduced a food donation (annadaan) scheme for devotees. We appealed to devotees to donate food on one day per year, on their birthday or the birthday or death anniversary of a loved one. The daily cost of serving food at the Prasadalaya comes to ₹5.5 lakh rupees. When a devotee donates this amount, the food served on that particular day is served in their name. Their name is displayed on TV screens in the Mandir and Prasadalaya. This scheme has garnered tremendous response. Devotees have donated the amount for food service for as many as 250 days in a year.

The growing number of visiting devotees is a challenge, and the Sansthan has brought in ultra-modern equipment to meet it. A system for cooking using solar energy had already been installed. Retrofittings on this system have been implemented. Thus, devotion is reinforced by technology and the devotees, for whom the act of eating prasad is also a form of worship, are satisfied. Daily, the work in the kitchen begins at 2 am and continues right up to 11 pm. It stops for only three hours every night, that too for the daily cleaning.

A visit to the Prasadalaya in Shirdi proves that even immense tasks become simple through the grace of Sai. Serving food to the hungry was a special aspect of Sai Baba's service. Even today, no one who visits the Prasadalaya goes away hungry.

From the beginning, the trustees have emphasised the use of latest technology for the efficient functioning of this mega kitchen. A large solar-steam cooking plant has been installed in the Prasadalaya, and 2,000 kg of food grains are cooked here daily. This plant, which was installed at the cost of ₹1.33 crores (₹13.3 million), has led to conservation of huge amounts of cooking gas. This project has received a grant from the Central Ministry of New and Renewable Energy. In addition to this, two containers with a capacity of 10 metric tonnes each have been installed to meet the daily requirement of cooking gas. An automatic chapati-making machine manufactured by Prama Kitchen Equipments has been installed to make chapatis. Three dough-kneading machines are used, each of them capable of kneading 40 kg of dough in 10 minutes. Before kneading, there are machines at every step—for clearing stones from wheat and for grinding wheat into flour. The entire system is such that one can pour wheat into the machines at one end and receive hot readymade chapatis brushed with ghee at the other end of the process.

Big machines have been installed to automate the processes of washing and chopping vegetables and cleaning the used plates and bowls. German dishwashers manufactured by Hobart have been installed. An ultra-modern fire-prevention security system has been installed in the kitchen. The quality and hygiene of food prepared is strictly controlled. Around 800 people are employed to work in the Prasadalaya.

Shirdi is now known world wide as devotees from every corner of the world visit. Sai Mandir has a special place in the hearts of the millions who visit every year. Shirdi is constantly setting new records vis-à-vis the number of visitors.

Ensuring easy, happy and smooth darshan for visiting devotees is the priority of the Sansthan. We place equal emphasis on ensuring that visiting devotees receive proper facilities and complete the pilgrimage to Shirdi in comfort. Devotees come to Shirdi from all parts of India. Many of them come from a poor background. It is important to provide them with good facilities for board and lodging. The trustees have faced this challenge with a positive attitude and detailed planning. We have set up the infrastructure to provide food and accommodation to the rapidly growing numbers. The most outstanding service is the Prasadalaya. The food served here is seen as the blessing of Sai Baba himself. His grace is such that any shortage is never experienced here. Sai Baba himself always cared for the hungry and feeding them was his unique trait. He would not eat his own meals unless he had fed the hungry—not just hungry people, but also cats and dogs. Donating food was a special aspect of his service. Even today, at Shirdi, we practise his mantra of donating food. Every devotee who eats at the Prasadalaya experiences divine satisfaction.

In most of the large temples in India, visiting devotees are served free-of-cost meals. This system is efficiently implemented at Shegaon and Akkalkot in Maharashtra. Implementing it at Shirdi was an immense challenge due to the sheer number of devotees visiting daily. But the trustees were determined to continue Baba's tradition of feeding the hungry and serving patients. So, we employed the latest technology and made continuous improvements for the benefit of the devotees. This facility is provided at the Mandir and at various points near the residential accommodations. In addition to feeding devotees, the Prasadalay also serves midday meals to thousands in old age homes and local schools for visually challenged and *divyang* students, which are located in and around Shirdi.

The newlyconstructed Prasadalaya, which cost around ₹22 crores (₹220 million), was dedicated to the public on 8 January 2009. Special dining halls have been constructed for devotees at the main Prasadalaya, Sai Baba Bhakta-niwas, Dwarawati Bhakta-niwas and Sai Ashram Bhakta-niwas. The main Prasadalaya as well as these dining halls serve meals from 10 am to 10 pm. A wholesome complete meal consisting of chapatis or puris, vegetables, rice, pulses, dal or sambar is served. This mega kitchen utilises around 30 quintals of rice and 40 quintals of wheat daily. Pulses, vegetables and other ingredients are used in proportionately large quantities.

The Prasadalaya has been awarded an ISO certification for maintaining quality and for efficient functioning. It is the first kitchen in Asia to receive this prestigious certificate. It has also received a special award from the Ministry of New and Renewable Energy in 2013 for being the largest solar energy project run by a religious institution. In 2013, the state government also presented the Sansthan with an award for energy conservation and promotion of solar energy. However, the true certificate of the efficiency of the Prasadalaya is the satisfaction on the faces of the devotees who eat here.

14

Sai Schools

Towards modernity through education

Education is given a special focus among the various initiatives run by Shri Sai Baba Sansthan. The school for girls, the English medium school for girls and boys, the ITI and the junior college have been offering education for many years. The degree college, with a faculty of arts, science and commerce, was also set up during this period. The development of a new modern educational complex, 7.0 lakh sq. ft. of construction with a project cost of ₹218 crores (₹2.18 billion), was also started. Currently, more than 6,000 students are studying in these institutions.

Through his own life, Sadguru Sai Baba created ideals of social service and education. Inspired by his ideals, the Sai Sansthan has fulfilled its social commitment by setting up model educational institutions. The schools and colleges managed by the Sansthan are making exemplary progress. Notably, the ITI has set new standards all over India.

I firmly believe that education is the only way one can shape the future. I myself was able to overcome challenging circumstances on the strength of my education. I sincerely wanted to provide the latest educational facilities to the students in the Shirdi area through the educational institutions. Shirdi was blessed by Sai Baba's residence, but it has remained underdeveloped in other aspects. I was confident that, given proper education, the residents of Shirdi would transform the face of the town. Hence, after darshan facilities and medical facilities, I focused my attention and efforts on the educational facilities.

The Sansthan has always prioritised educational initiatives. The Sansthan, at present, runs five educational institutions in Shirdi—Shri Sai Baba Kanya Vidyamandir (a girls' school), Shri Sai Baba English Medium School (junior kindergarten to Standard X), Junior College, Industrial Training Institute (ITI) and degree college.

Currently, more than 6,000 students are studying in these institutions. They are receiving high-quality education at very low costs. The poor and needy are benefiting greatly from this initiative. At present, the colleges of the Sansthan function in the premises of the Dharmashala.

I envisioned a well-equipped modern educational complex in Shirdi and I began to take planned steps towards achieving this goal. The Board of Trustees decided that, in order to provide students with a conducive atmosphere for quality education, a modern educational complex should be set up. I had the vision of a single educational complex housing the schools, colleges, ITI, library, laboratory, hostel, playground and auditorium. A budget of ₹218 crores (₹2.18 billion) has been set aside for this project and 18 acres of land earmarked for the complex. The project design has been prepared. The work order for the same has also been issued after completing a transparent e-tender process. The construction is in an advanced stage and is expected to be completed by March 2021.

This complex has spacious buildings to house all the necessary institutions, including a separate school for girls, a well-stocked library, fully equipped laboratories, a playground for sports, a swimming pool, facilities for indoor games, a teachers' common room, an auditorium with a seating capacity of 1,050 and a separate hall for educational and cultural activities. This complex will aim at widening the horizons of knowledge and science. Students from the surrounding areas will benefit from these facilities. They will get significant opportunities to excel at education as well as in sports.

The degree college managed by the Sansthan has started functioning and was the first significant necessary step in the direction of educational progress. I also proposed setting up a free-of-cost training centre in Shirdi for UPSC/MPSC competitive exams. The building is ready and the centre, which is for students from rural areas, is expected to become functional soon.

Hon. Prime Minister Shri Narendra Modi visited Shirdi on 19 October 2018 to lay the foundation stone of the modern educational complex project spread over 18 acres of land and having a built-up area of around 7.0 lakh sq.ft. The Hon. PM took a detailed survey of the proposed plans for the same. This project is rapidly taking shape.

Shri Sai Baba Sansthan planted the seeds of education in a small town that did not have access to many facilities. The newly opened degree college has three faculties—arts, science and commerce. Even after sustained efforts by many over 15 years, the vision of this degree college did not become a reality. The Board of Trustees, particularly Vice President Mr Chandrashekhar Kadam and other senior officials, took untiring efforts. With orders from the then Chief Minister Hon. Shri Devendra Fadnavis and the then Education Minister Hon. Shri Vinod Tawde, the degree college was opened in 2018. These educational institutions have created a unique identity by offering high-quality education.

Sai Baba came to a small town like Shirdi and as a result, Shirdi was transformed. Baba set ideals of social service, education and healthcare, thereby inspiring lakhs of devotees to follow in his footsteps. The combined efforts of skilled administrators and dedicated teachers helped in the growth of the sapling that Sai Baba planted.

Industrial Training Institute (ITI)

The ITI managed by Sai Baba Sansthan occupies the pride of place among all the educational institutions. Under the leadership of Principal Shivalinga Patne, students have established new records and have won renown at the national level. Shri Sai Baba ITI was established on 1 August 1984. This government-recognised institute is regarded as being top-ranking among private industrial training institutes. It has received the 'A' grade among private institutes.

From four initial trades, the ITI now offers training for 11 trades such as electrician, mechanic motor vehicle, mechanic tractor, fitter, welder, turner, mechanic RAC, tool and die maker, computer operator, programming assistant and machinist grinder as well as training in the fields of information technology and communication system maintenance. There are 22 divisions for these trades, and training is given in two shifts. Two workshops are set up for the trainees to perform practicals. The institute has seats for 450 trainees. All admissions are conducted online and on merit basis as per the norms of the state government. Due to the online system, there is no scope for favouritism or nepotism in the admission process. I am proud to state that the educational institutions in Shirdi are free from corruption.

Compared to other educational institutions, the fees charged by Sansthan are very low. The state government norms allow a 20 per cent management quota, but these management seats are also transferred to the government and all admissions are made as per common rules. As much as 90 per cent of the successful students get a placement. This is probably the only ITI where graduates get a placement.

In 2013–2014, the government increased tuition fees, but the Sai Baba ITI retained its old fee structure. As a result, the Sansthan gives a total fee waiver of around ₹92 lakhs (₹9.2 million) to trainees every year.

Since 2001, the ITI has received the 'A' grade. In 2004, the institute was ranked second in the state of Maharashtra. In 2005 and 2006, the institute progressed to the first rank in the state. From 2006 till date, the institute has won the national-level Best Institute Award by the central government a total number of seven times, and 21 trainees of the institute have ranked first in the state of Maharashtra, 12 students qualified for all-India level training and seven have bagged first rank at the national level. The first three toppers were felicitated by the state government with an award of ₹10,000/- each. The four subsequent toppers were honoured as 'Best Artisan of India' with an award of ₹50,000/- each by the central government. The credit for this achievement goes to the hard work by the talented students and the focused guidance given by the dedicated teachers. These achievements have boosted everybody's enthusiasm.

Thirty Crores for Classrooms in Zilla Parishad Schools

Shri Sai Baba Sansthan granted ₹30 crores (₹300 million) for developing classrooms in zilla parishad schools of Ahmednagar district. The working of the Sansthan is primarily based on the spirit of social service. This very spirit has inspired the educational services by the Sansthan. I feel a deep sense of satisfaction for having accomplished a major task in the field of education. However, only education would not have sufficed—there was a need to lead Sai devotees towards modernisation.

3. SAI DARSHAN

15

Samadhi Shatabdi

A unique event of my life

The Sai Samadhi Centenary Celebration was the most challenging event during my tenure as the chairman. With the inauguration of the year-long event by Hon. President of India Shri Ramnath Kovind, the international airport at Shirdi was also opened. Around 4 crores (40 million) of devotees visited Shirdi during this period. Distinguished guests visited Shirdi almost daily. The concluding ceremony was graced by Hon. Prime Minister of India Shri Narendra Modi. The organisation and management of this celebration was a testing experience for us.

I believe that the Sai Samadhi Centenary Year occurring during my tenure is the most fortunate and important event in my life. A celebration that takes place once in a hundred years! The opportunity to manage this event as the chairman was itself a blessing from Sai Baba. In a way, it was a testing time for me. The celebrations were to continue throughout the year, and many dignitaries were expected to visit Shirdi. So, it was quite a challenge. I have always enjoyed taking up challenges. I resolved to make the centenary celebrations both grand and memorable. To take up this Herculean task, I decided to rely on my colleagues from the Sansthan Trust, the chief executive officer, other administrative officers, all the employees, devotees and villagers too. Fortunately, I received excellent cooperation from all of them. We meticulously planned all the events for the entire year. We took care to maintain the grandeur of the various events organised. The enthusiasm of the devotees knew no bounds.

Inauguration Ceremony

The Shri Sai Baba Samadhi Centenary Celebrations were organised by the Shri Sai Baba Sansthan Trust in the period from 1 October 2017 to 18 October 2018. Both were Baba's samadhi days, which falls on Dussehra day. During this period, the Sansthan organised activities based on the 5-Point Programme—religious, cultural, social service, creating public awareness and paduka darshan. Also, important projects and initiatives were launched to provide various facilities for the devotees who would visit Shirdi for the Shri Sai Baba Samadhi Centenary. These facilities were created not just for the centenary year, but with a long-term purpose.

The Shri Sai Baba Samadhi Centenary Celebrations were inaugurated by none other than the Hon. President of India Shri Ramnath Kovind at 11.00 am on 1 October 2017. A pooja with chanting of Vedic mantras was performed, and the sacred saffron flag on the specially built centenary dhwaj-stambh (flag post) was hoisted by the President in Lendi Baug in the temple premises. The day of the inauguration ceremony was also the President's birthday. I made a special mention of this during my brief address and offered best wishes to him on behalf of all of us. We are indeed fortunate that the samadhi centenary of Shri Sai Baba has occurred during our lifetime. It was celebrated in India and all over the world with great enthusiasm. The centenary was celebrated in all the 8,450 Sai Baba temples. The 'Sai App' was launched on this occasion to make facilities such as live darshan, literature, darshan pass, room booking, donations online.

The President spoke at length about the teachings of Sai Baba. He expressed happiness about the planning of the year-long celebrations and proudly declared that he is a Sai devotee by heart and visits Shirdi every year. He said if you look in any direction in Shirdi, you will find only Sai. Be it a hotel, restaurant, general shop or store, you will find that it is named after Sai. Sai Baba's teachings are highly relevant these days and are of eternal significance. The number of people coming to Shirdi is increasing day by day. The Sansthan has been very well developed in receiving those many devotees to Shirdi and to give them a satisfying experience and emphasised the need to make Shirdi a clean town. He attended the ceremony with all his family members. He was very pleased to be in the presence of Sai Baba in Shirdi, especially on the occasion of his birthday.

He wrote in the visitor's register: 'I consider myself indeed blessed by inaugurating the Sai Baba's samadhi centenary celebrations. Baba's mantra of shraddha and saburi and sab ka mailk ek are boons to humanity. I wish that Shirdi emerges as the centre for the welfare of humanity and its fragrance spreads everywhere.'

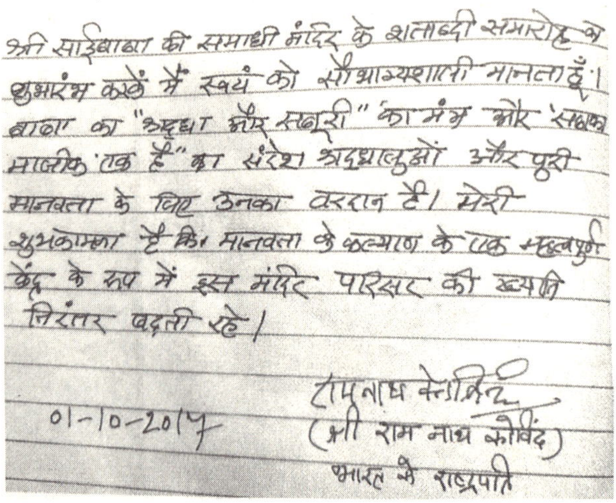
श्री साईबाबा की समाधी मंदिर के शताब्दी समारोह के
शुभारंभ करके मैं स्वयं को सौभाग्यशाली मानता हूँ।
बाबा का "श्रद्धा और सबूरी" का मंत्र और 'सबका
मालिक एक है" का संदेश श्रद्धालुओं और पूरी
मानवता के लिए उनका वरदान है। मेरी
शुभकामना है कि मानवता के कल्याण के एक महत्वपूर्ण
केंद्र के रूप में इस मंदिर परिसर की ख्याति
निरंतर बढ़ती रहे।

रामनाथ कोविन्द
01-10-2017
(श्री राम नाथ कोविंद)
भारत के राष्ट्रपति

Message by President of India Hon'ble Shri Ramnath Kovind in the visitors' book of the Sai Baba Sansthan, Shirdi

I outlined the 5-Point Programme, the guiding principles of the activities to be carried out during the centenary year, during my speech.

The 5-Point Programme

1. Religious festivals: Dussehra, Ram Navami, Guru Purnima and other religious occasions were celebrated at a larger scale than the usual celebrations.

2. Social service: Food donation, blood donation, organ donation, eye donation, healthcare activities, tree plantation, cleanliness drives, etc. were carried out. Sai Baba Hospital and Sainath Hospital organised various medical camps: 1) Eye Check-up and Free Spectacles Distribution Camp; 2) Cataract and Strabismus Surgery Camp; 3) Mega Blood Donation Camp; 4) Kidney Stone Treatment Camp; 5) Jaipur Foot (prosthetic foot) Camp; 6) Prosthetic Arm Camp; 7) Dental Check-up Camp; 8) Rhinoplasty Camp; 9) Surgery for Burns Victims Camp; 10) Elephantiasis Treatment Camp; 11) Ear Nose Throat (ENT) and Hearing-aid Instrument Distribution Camp; 12) Cancer Diagnosis Camp 13) One-day General Diagnostic Camp. Thousands of patients benefited through these camps.
3. Cultural programmes: Organising bhajan evenings, keertan, religious discourses, devotional music and songs, etc.
4. Creating public awareness: Many events were conducted in various fields. The grand Dhyan Shibir (meditation camp) by Shri Shivakrupanand Swami was attended by 20,000 devotees from 15 Indian states and 22 countries. The zero-budget natural farming camp by Padmashri Subhash Palekar was attended by 6,000 young farmers. The grand Sai Satcharitra Mahaparayan week was attended by 12,000 devotees. The International Sai Mandir Parishad (conference) was attended by 4,000 dignitaries. The All-India Tribal Conference was attended by 3,000 tribals from all states in India

and the Akhand Harinam Saptah was attended by one lakh devotees.

5. Sai Paduka Darshan programmes: The original charma paduka (leather footwear) of Sai Baba were taken to every district in Maharashtra and most of the states in India, from Kashmir to Kanyakumari and from Kutch to Kamrup. We also planned to take the paduka to different countries across the world, but the logistics could not be worked out.

The Concluding Ceremony of the Celebrations

On 19 October 2018, the closing ceremony of the centenary year was successfully completed at the hands of the Hon. Prime Minister Shri Narendra Modi. Bhoomi-poojan of various new projects by the Sansthan was performed, and the commemorative silver coin for the Shri Sai Baba Samadhi Centenary Year Celebrations was released. The then Governor Hon. Shri C. Vidyasagar Rao and the then Chief Minister Hon. Shri Devendra Fadnavis also graced the occasion with their presence. Bhoomi-poojan of five major projects worth ₹575 crores (₹57.5 million) was performed by the Hon. Prime Minister of India Shri Narendra Modi.

Modi ji gave an inspiring speech on this occasion and the core ideas of his speech were spiritual. He quoted a number of historical incidents. Every word he spoke was a testimony to the sincere devotion he cherishes towards Sai Baba. The presence of our deeply devout prime minister lent a positive energy to the entire temple premises. He praised various social, educational, spiritual and healthcare initiatives of the Sansthan. Modi ji wrote thus in a visitor's book: 'Sai Baba's message of shraddha and saburi is an inspiration to entire humanity. I am feeling extreme peace upon taking the darshan of Sai Baba. You can experience an atmosphere of true secularity in Shirdi. Keeping aside their religious differences everybody bows his head at the feet of Baba. His mahamantra of "sab ka mailk ek" has great importance in achieving world peace, in the current scenario. I wish all devotees to receive His choicest blessings and may they get happiness and peace. With this I again bow my head on the feet of Sai Baba.'

While in the temple, Modi ji called every trustee and officer to him and said, 'Sai ke darbar mein sab barabar hai.' I was asked for some inputs to be included in the speech of the Hon. Prime Minister. This is the normal practice whenever dignitaries visit the place. I gave my input in Marathi, 'Shraddha asudya ani saburi pan theva. Sarvana Babancha Ashirwad milo hi mi saicharani prarthana karto', meaning, 'Have devotion and have patience too. I pray at the feet of Sai Baba that we all may receive His blessings.' I was waiting for the prime minister to say this throughout his speech, but he had chosen it to conclude his talk. I was delighted when he ended his speech with the words I had supplied.

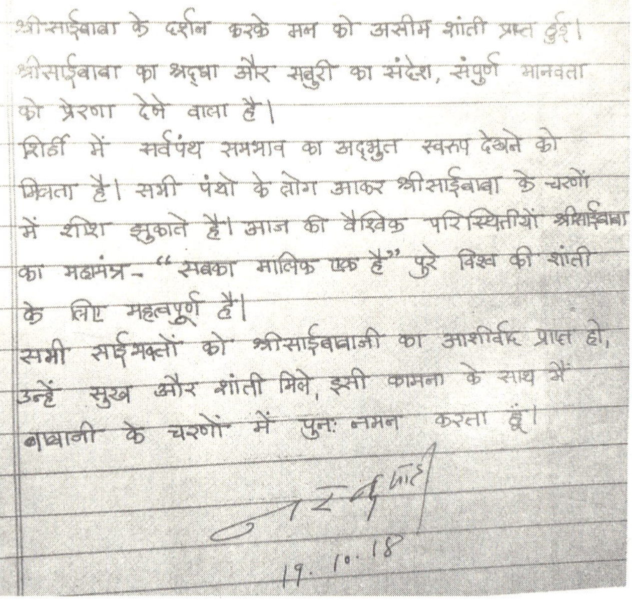

श्रीसाईबाबा के दर्शन करके मन को असीम शांती प्राप्त हुई।
श्रीसाईबाबा का श्रद्धा और सबुरी का संदेश, संपुर्ण मानवता
को प्रेरणा देने वाला है।
शिर्डी में सर्वपंथ समभाव का अद्भुत स्वरूप देखने को
मिलता है। सभी पंथो के लोग आकर श्रीसाईबाबा के चरणों
में शीश झुकाते है। आज की वैश्विक परिस्थितीयों श्रीसाईबाबा
का महामंत्र- "सबका मालिक एक है" पुरे विश्व की शांती
के लिए महत्वपूर्ण है।
सभी साईभक्तों को श्रीसाईबाबाजी का आशीर्वाद प्राप्त हो,
उन्हें सुख और शांती मिले, इसी कामना के साथ मैं
बाबाजी के चरणों में पुनः नमन करता हूं।

नरेन्द्र मोदी
19. 10. 18

Message by Prime Minister of India Hon. Shri Narendra Modi in the visitor's book of Sai Baba Sansthan Shirdi

Global Sai Temple Summit

The Hon. Vice President of India Shri Venkaiah Naidu was in Shirdi on 23 December 2017 to attend and address the Global Sai Temple Summit. It was attended by around 4,000 Sai temple trustees from 22 countries. Venkaiah ji's speech was spontaneous. He spoke in five languages, Hindi, English, Telugu, Sanskrit and Marathi. The speech was so powerful that the entire audience was mesmerised.

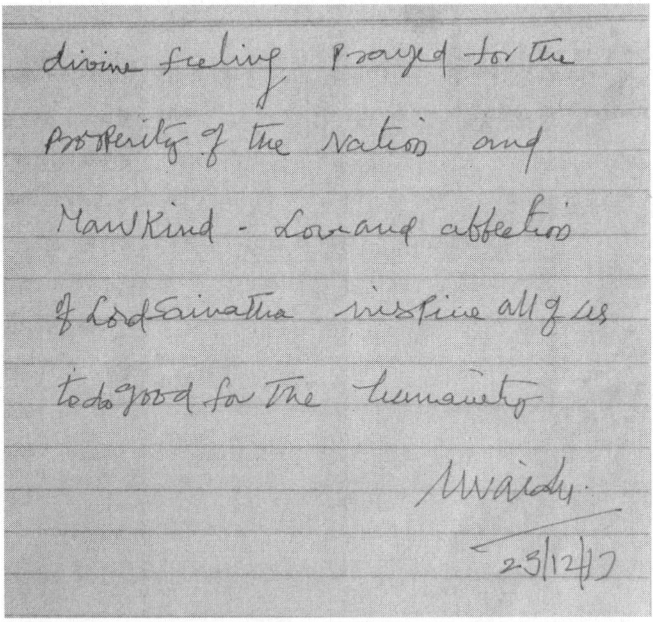

divine feeling prayed for the prosperity of the nation and Mankind - Love and affection of Lord Sainatha inspire all of us to do good for The humanity

M Naidu.

23/12/17

'Divine feeling. Prayed for the prosperity of the nation and mankind. Love and affection of Lord Sainath inspire all of us to do good for the humanity.'

Message by Hon. Shri Venkaiah Naidu, Vice President of India in the visitor's book of Sai Baba Sansthan, Shirdi

Gangagiri Maharaj Saptah

The Sarsanghchalak (Chief) of RSS, Dr Mohan Bhagwat, participated in the Gangagiri Maharaj Saptah on 22 August 2018, which was organised as a mass education programme. While in the temple, he also visited the blood donation centre and expressed satisfaction over the fact that the face of Sai Baba temple is becoming socially oriented.

He wrote in the visitor's register: 'It is pleasing to know that Shri Sai Baba temple has started taking care of all the facets of the society upon becoming an important centre of the society. By putting into practice the mantra of Sai Baba, that of shraddha-saburi and sab ka mailk ek, the Sansthan will expand its horizon of service and devotion. I congratulate all the trustees and wish for a better future for them.'

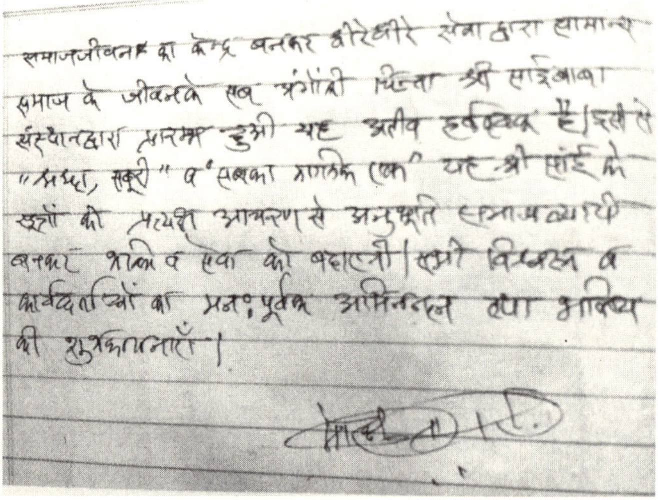

समाजजीवन का केन्द्र बनकर धीरे धीरे सेवा द्वारा सामान्य
समाज के जीवन के सब अंगों की चिंता श्री साईबाबा
संस्थान द्वारा प्रारम्भ हुई यह अतीव हर्षवर्धक है। इसी से
"श्रद्धा, सबूरी" व 'सबका मालिक एक' यह श्री साईं के
सूत्रों की प्रत्यक्ष आचरण से अनुभूति समाजव्यापी
बनकर भक्ति व सेवा को बढ़ायेगी। सभी विश्वस्त व
कार्यकर्ताओं का मनःपूर्वक अभिनन्दन तथा भविष्य
की शुभकामनाएँ।

Message by Sarsanghchalak (Chief) of RSS Dr Mohan Bhagwat in the visitor's book of Sai Baba Sansthan, Shirdi

In addition to these, a number of dignitaries from central/state ministries and celebrities from Bollywood and all other fields poured in all over the year. The year of the samadhi centenary was full of activities. It was a very satisfying year.

16

Sai Darshan

Mothers with infants to get direct darshan

One scene in particular affected me deeply. In the midst of the queue, a lady was perched on a bench, hiding her face while she breastfed her infant. She was embarrassed by the crowd of men around her. She could not let her infant go hungry, nor could she give up her place in the queue for darshan. The anguish of this mother disquieted me, and I thought that things should be changed urgently. There was a dire need for some basic and long-term facilities. I immediately decided that mothers with infants would be exempted from the queue and be allowed to get direct darshan. I also set up breastfeeding rooms for mothers. A similar facility for direct darshan was provided for senior citizens, for devotees with medical conditions and handicaps. They too were exempted from the queue.

I took charge as the chairman of the Sansthan and came to Shirdi. When I entered the town, I once again experienced the same lack of discipline and uncontrolled crowding. I went to the temple and directly joined the queue for darshan. People were crowding, pushing and shoving and using influence to get ahead in the queue.

Employees who recognised me stared at me in surprise. Never before had they seen a chairman who waited in the queue for darshan! While I progressed in the queue, I carefully observed the conditions around me. The discomforts faced by the devotees who had travelled hundreds of miles to get Sai Darshan pained me. I could see crowding, unbearable heat, shortage of drinking water and inconvenience to babies, children and the aged. Agents were openly defying rules by trading VIP Darshan passes and fleecing genuine devotees. All these things distressed me.

I keenly felt the need to address the poor conditions in the queue for darshan. Being a scientist, I pondered how technology could be used to address these problems.

When I reflected on what my primary duty as the chairman of the Sai Baba Sansthan was, I realised that it was to ensure a hassle-free and pleasant Sai Darshan experience for devotees. Board and lodging are supplementary facilities—the primary focus should be a pleasant darshan experience.

That first day, I somehow managed to get darshan and reached my office. The very first decision I took in the capacity of chairman was regarding the queue for darshan. To ensure proper ventilation, I doubled the number of fans in the queue area. Replacing the old-fashioned windows with big glass-paned ones ensured adequate light for the devotees. We also added air-conditioning in the queue halls.

We provided a free-of-cost supply of tea, coffee, milk and biscuits to the devotees waiting in the queue and stopped the sale of bottled water taking place. An RO water purification plant was installed, and pure drinking water was made available to all the devotees free of cost. The toilets in this area were absolutely filthy. We arranged for the cleaning of these toilets at regular intervals and retiled them for cleanliness and better appearance.

Since a large number of devotees visit Shirdi daily, they have to wait in the queue for many hours to get darshan. To utilise this waiting time effectively, we installed more than 250 LED closed-circuit TV monitors along the darshan queue. They would run a live telecast of the Sai idol, pooja, aarti, keertan and pravachan. The devotees would get absorbed in the spiritual content being telecast and their waiting period would become more bearable.

I would like to share with you my personal experience. Once, a large group of visually impaired people visited the mandir for darshan. They expressed their joy and satisfaction at being allowed to take darshan directly, having been exempted from the queue. Somebody asked them, 'You are unable to see Baba, then what did you gain by coming all the way here for darshan?' The reply that one of them gave truly opened my eyes. He said, 'It is true that we cannot see Baba, but isn't it sufficient that Baba can see us? It is enough for us that His gracious vision fell on us.'

Computerised Time Slot Darshan Facility

Basic improvements such as making the queue for darshan congenial and reducing the waiting time spent by devotees were the need of the hour. With this in mind, I studied the darshan queue systems at various popular places of worship in India. I harnessed the latest technology and employed a computerised biometric time slot system for darshan. To implement this system, around 40 computers were set up at various points around the mandir area. The devotee is registered first—a computerised photograph is clicked and fingerprint impressions are recorded. Then they are issued a pass for darshan with a time slot. Devotees can obtain this pass as soon as they arrive in Shirdi. They are then allotted a fixed time slot for darshan, so that they can manage the rest of their schedule and arrive in the darshan queue at the given time. While joining the queue, every pass is scanned. It is also scanned at the exit after darshan, so that a record of the time required to obtain darshan for each devotee is maintained. It was found that on an average, it takes around 45 minutes for the devotee to get darshan. And they need not stand in queues for six or seven hours any more. The system works on the estimation that an average of 6,000 devotees get darshan every hour. Another advantage of this system was that we could record the exact number of visiting devotees. Earlier, these numbers would only be estimates.

This was a revolutionary change that we introduced. Now, an online booking facility has also been made available for visiting devotees.

The Sai Baba Sansthan Mandir was awarded the ISO certification by the government for excellent management. As a result, the facilities for pooja and other rituals have been authenticated and standardised.

Making VIP Darshan Open to All

I took charge with the determination to bring in transparent functioning in all systems. One negative aspect about Shirdi had caught my attention as soon as I had arrived. In a way, unsuspecting devotees were being looted. There was a facility to obtain a VIP pass for immediate darshan by donating ₹200/- to the mandir. However, for this VIP pass, one also required a letter of recommendation from an MLA, MLC, MP, minister or a local leader. A whole gang of agents supplying such letters of recommendation would move around the mandir area. They would target unsuspecting devotees and fleece them of hundreds of rupees in exchange for these letters. They would charge ₹1,000/- for the pass that cost only ₹200/-. They were running a wide and well-entrenched racket. The Public Relations Office, where such passes were issued, would always be crowded with agents. I immediately resolved to do away with the requirement of any recommendation letter for obtaining a VIP darshan pass. A number of people, including some officials, warned me, 'Do not take such a decision. It will have negative effects; you will face tremendous opposition.' In a way, they attempted to pressure me into changing my mind, but I did not pay heed to them. I believed that the fleecing of devotees must be stopped, and I took a firm stand. I took the trustees into confidence and stopped this harmful practice. I removed the necessity of recommendation letters for getting a VIP darshan pass, thus making the facility available to all.

I ordered that the paid VIP passes be made available on demand to anyone. Online booking of such passes was also started. This proved to be a boon for devotees who are pressed for time. The agents crowding around the Public Relations Office disappeared. I was waiting for a backlash, but no one opposed me. Many people were worried that such a step might affect the revenue flowing into the Sansthan. In actual fact, the mandir was earning around ₹18 crores (₹180 million) annually through the sale of VIP passes. In the first year after my decision, the revenue jumped to ₹43 crores (₹430 million), and in the year after that, it reached ₹61 crores (₹610 million). Thus, the huge amounts of money which were being diverted from mandir revenues were secured. I was successful in curbing the loot of devotees and the rampant corruption being carried out in the name of VIP darshan.

When the VIP pass facility was offered to the public, in the first year, 21.5 lakh (2.15 million) devotees benefited from it. In the next year, 30.5 lakh (3.05 million) devotees opted for these passes. Under this facility, devotees can obtain darshan within 15 to 20 minutes. Now, while booking railway tickets to Shirdi from anywhere in the country, devotees can also book a darshan time slot. This facility is being offered in cooperation with the railways. Thousands of devotees avail this facility.

Modern Darshan Queue Complex Project

In consultation with the trustees, we prepared a plan to improve the darshan facilities. This plan was named the Modern Darshan Queue Complex. In order to make the Sai Darshan process pleasant and comfortable for devotees, the Sansthan is building a well-equipped fully air-conditioned Darshan Queue Complex at the location of the old Prasadalaya. The main building of the Darshan Queue Complex will occupy an area of 20,082 sq. mtrs. The ground floor will have an area of 6,581 sq. mtrs., while both the first and second floors will have an area of 6,133 sq. mtrs. each. This building will contain three large entrance halls that will be wellequipped with facilities such as mobile phone and footwear storage lockers, 48 biometric pass issue counters, 20 paid pass issue counters, 10 counters for sale of ladoos, 10 counters for udi (sacred ash) and kapad-kothi, 10 bookstalls, a donation office, a tea and coffee counter, separate washrooms for men and women, spacious lifts, R.O.-purified drinking water, proper ventilation, fire-fighting equipment, a security check, etc. This building will contain a total of 12 halls, which will be able to accommodate a total of 18,000 devotees. This project has an estimated cost of ₹110 crores (₹1.10 billion) and the work is at an advanced stage. This complex is connected directly to the mandir through a skywalk.

Mukh Darshan Facility

Every devotee longs for darshan, but not all have enough time. These are the devotees who fall prey to corrupt rackets. Having observed this, I contemplated a solution to the problem. The idea of introducing Mukh

Darshan suddenly came to mind. Devotees who were pressed for time could avail the joy of Mukh Darshan at least. So, I made arrangements for the same at the front of the mandir.

I had presented a request to the Minister for Railways, Mr Piyush Goyal, that the devotees travelling to Shirdi by train should be allowed to book darshan passes at the time of booking their travel tickets. Mr Goyal immediately granted the request. Due to his speedy implementation, this facility was offered to devotees starting from 26 January 2019. Around 57 trains arrive or pass through Shirdi station every week. Now all the devotees travelling by these trains can book darshan passes along with the railway tickets.

17

Sai Sangam—Shirdi

Devotion to Sai Baba has transcended national borders

There are many Sai temples in India and abroad. I envisioned a network that would bring together all these Sai temples. I expressed a desire that Sai temples all over the world should work for society with a common aim to promote social responsibility in all their activities. To accomplish this, we organised two international conferences at Shirdi for the trustees of Sai temples all over the world. Both were well attended, with the participation of Sai devotees from 22 countries. Hon. Venkaiah Naidu, Vice President of India, addressed the conference.

The family of Sai devotees is the largest group of devotees in the world. No other modern saint has so many temples built in their honour all over the world. There are more than 450 Sai temples in countries other than India. The USA alone has 80 Sai temples, Malaysia 22, the UK 5 and so on. A total of 43 countries such as Germany, France, Japan, Australia, New Zealand and Switzerland have Sai temples. And there are around 8,000 Sai temples in India. Nearly half of these are located in Andhra Pradesh and Telangana. It is to be noted that these are considerably big temples and primarily Sai temples. Thus, the Sai Movement is international. These temples have a number of common features. Therefore, I desired that there should be a common association of all the Sai temples and that they should coordinate their activities.

I aimed at defining a common mission—making these temples more oriented towards the devotees and towards service to society. With this aim, we organised the first international conference of the Sai temple trustees from all over India and the world on 11 and 12 December 2016 at Shirdi. The conference received an enthusiastic response. On 23 December 2017, the second international conference of Sai Mandir trustees was also successfully organised in the Sai Mandir premises. Hon. Vice President of India Shri Venkaiah Naidu graced the occasion with his presence. These conferences were attended by 4,000 trustees of around 1,028 Sai temples from 24 states of India and from 22 other countries.

While addressing the participants, I explained the rationale behind my idea of organising the conference. This international conference of Sai temple trustees was probably the first effort of its kind. We deliberated on how to create coordination between various temples and how to make their initiatives more oriented towards service to society. We also exchanged ideas on the planning and implementation of common initiatives across the world. The five initiatives—blood donation, educational activities, healthcare services, organ donation and food donation—were resolved as mandatory for the temples. We also announced five additional activities, which can be taken up depending on local needs—eradication of illiteracy, poverty alleviation, eradication of superstition, organising yoga camps and environmental initiatives. We also resolved to maintain basic uniformity in the poojas and aartis performed. I am happy to share that the Sai temple at Shirdi has been awarded the ISO certification. The detailed rituals of the pooja and aartis performed at Shirdi temple and the details of the prasad are easily available on the temple website. People can use them to ensure that uniform pooja rituals are performed in all the Sai temples

Another aim of the conference was to connect all the Sai temples in the world with the main temple at Shirdi, which is the powerhouse for all these temples and trustees. Shirdi is a sangam place, just like Prayag-teerth (a meeting place of the holy rivers of Ganga, Yamuna and Saraswati) in India or the Vatican in Europe, for all the Sai temples.

It was wonderful to listen to Shri Venkaiah ji Naidu. He spoke to the audience in five languages—Sanskrit, Telugu, Hindi, English and Marathi. His words touched people's hearts. He spoke spontaneously and did not deliver a written speech like most dignitaries. He touched hearts because he was speaking from the heart. The audience was immersed in his speech.

I believe that the family of Sai devotees is the largest group of its kind in the world. No other movement has so many followers. When I reflected on who was the founder of this huge movement, I realised that there is no defined leader for this immense family. There is no single person who has travelled all over India and the world to establish Sai temples. Also, no one travelled from Shirdi to all these places with the aim of establishing temples. Therefore, one has to conclude that the mover and promoter of this immense movement is none other than Sai Baba himself. Various devotees had divine experiences of Sai Baba and were motivated to establish Sai temples. The number of temples began to increase, and they became popular of their own accord. We believed that this movement across the world should become more organised and should have a proper management.

Sai Baba has taught us by leading Himself in the service to the society. If we want to worship Sai Baba, we must do it through the act of social service, which He will like most.

I am confident that through the efforts of Sai Sevaks, Sai devotees and Sai temples, no resident of the respective locality will go hungry and everyone will have access to education and healthcare services. Through these initiatives, the Sai devotee movement will touch the hearts of the people. I envision that all the Sai temples in the world will join this movement.

The conference was highly successful. It was my sincere effort to bring together the Sai temples from all over the world. The response we received was overwhelming. Participants expressed their satisfaction, saying that they had been coming to Shirdi all these years, but this time Baba had called them to Shirdi. It was a memorable event, and people will cherish the memories for a long time.

18

Sai Mandir

Not just a temple, it's a movement

The Sai Mandir at Shirdi is not just a Sai Baba Samadhi Mandir—it has many aspects. When you visit Shirdi next time, try to see and visit all these places. You will be mesmerised. The Sai Movement started from here is now the largest in the world.

The Saibaba Sansthan Shirdi is the second-largest temple in India. The Sansthan was first registered/formed on 13 February 1922 with an order of the District Court of Ahmednagar. Dasganu Maharaj was the first Chairman of the Sansthan[34]. It is now governed by 'The Shri Saibaba Sansthan Trust Act—2004' under the aegis of the Government of Maharashtra, which appoints the board of trustees.

1. *Samadhi Mandir:* This was called Buti Wada as it was built by Gopal, the alias of Bapusaheb Buti of Nagpur (Maharashtra) in the year 1917–1918. It was built with the permission of Sai Baba and was proposed to be the Krishna Mandir. The idol of Murlidhar (now placed in the museum) was brought in for the installation. Those days Baba used to

reside for most of the time in Dwarkamai. He would visit Buti Wada every day on His way to Lendi Baug and inspect the work, advise changes, etc. The construction work of Buti Wada was nearing completion as Baba's health deteriorated. The day of his samadhi was approaching. And ultimately, on the day of Dussehra of 1918, i.e., 15 October, at 2.30 pm, Tuesday, He took Mahasamadhi. Before that he had instructed that he should be taken to Buti Wada. After His Samadhi, there were differences between local Hindus and Muslims regarding the final abode of Baba. The matter was sent to the district collector, but finally all the devotees decided to take Him to Buti Wada and that became His final abode. Buti Wada was converted into the Samadhi Mandir. Initially, only the photo of Sai Baba was placed at the site of His samadhi. Later, in 1954, His idol (murti) was installed. The story of Baba's murti is interesting and is narrated in a separate chapter in this book. The golden sinhasan and the decoration were installed subsequently on 23 December 2007. The Samadhi Mandir has a small basement and one upper floor. The building, made entirely of stone, is now more than a hundred years old. Though it looks strong, it needs to be structurally analysed and retrofitted, as per the changes in the construction technology over the last hundred years. When you visit Shirdi, you can see this heritage structure, which has been preserved. It was named Buti Wada, but that name was not used for a number of years. Buti's heirs were following up with this matter with the Sansthan without success. It was in my tenure as chairman that the name 'Buti Wada' was reinstalled on the building of the Samadhi Mandir.

2. *Devotee Photos:* Inside the Samadhi Mandir, on the upper side of the Sabha Mandap, you will find some photographs. Do look at them while in the queue for Baba's darshan. They feature the staunch devotees of Baba—Nanasaheb Chandorkar, Annasaheb Dabholkar, Balasaheb Bhate, Nanasaheb Nimonkar, Bapusaheb Buti, Mhalsapati Bhagat, Bayjabai Kote Patil, Kakasaheb Dixit, Tatya Ganpat Kote Patil, Dasganu Maharaj, Bhagoji Shinde, Kashiram Bala Shimpi, Laxman Ganesh Noolkar, Laxmibai Shinde, Madhavrao Deshpande, Moreshwar Pradhan and so on. More photographs have been added later[30].
3. *Sathe and Navalkar Wada:* Rao Bahadur H.V. Sathe was the district deputy collector of Ahmednagar in 1904. He erected the Sathe Wada in 1908 adjoining the Buti Wada and the covering neem tree and Guru Sthan. This was as per Baba's own instructions, and it was probably the first lodging facility for devotees in those days. It was later purchased by Shri Ramkrishna Shrikrishna Navalkar and came to be known as Navalkar Wada. Traditionally, wadas are named after their owners. Later this wada was demolished and the space was cleared and hence it cannot be seen there[30].
4. *Mandir Kalash:* Kalash is a metal or stone spire used to top the gopur (dome) of Hindu temples. It is an indication of the logical completion of the temple. It is the topmost point of the temple. A kalash with a gold covering was installed in Shirdi on 29 September 1952 and the shikhara (spire) portion,

above the samadhi place of the temple, was covered with gold on 26 July 2007[34].

5. *Neem Tree:* As you come out of the Samadhi Mandir after taking Baba's darshan, you will see a big neem tree. This tree has been there since Baba's days. The specialty of this neem tree is that the leaves of one of its branches are not bitter. Devotees call it sweet with devotion and love though it is not really sweet, but the taste is not bitter either. The leaves of this tree are considered sacred and you will find devotees collecting the fallen leaves and taking them home. The importance of this tree is first that Baba used to sit under it for a long time and practise meditation and second, the Guru Sthan is located under this tree. There is a passage to walk around the tree (pradakshina). During the samadhi centenary year, we successfully employed tissue culture on this special branch of the neem tree and created hundreds of plants, which were donated to the devotees and the dignitaries. Sai temples across the globe could be given trees with one such tissue culture neem plant.
6. *Guru Sthan:* Below the neem tree, the guru of Sai Baba has a place. Earlier Baba used to sit and meditate here. Once he told people that this is the place of his guru. He also asked people to dig up the spot and when they did, it is reported that they found a burning lamp there. This place is known as Guru Sthan. Sai Baba's photo and paduka are installed there.
7. *Dwarkamai:* This is the place where Baba used to stay. It was an abandoned and old masjid. No namaz

was offered there. It was in a dilapidated state, but Baba cleaned it and chose to make it his place to meet devotees and also to sleep. It can be called his control room. He named it Dwarkamai. There is a dhuni (fire) which has been continuously lit since the times of Baba. It still burns 24x7. Udi (sacred ash) is produced from this dhuni. There is a grinder and a jute sack full of wheat. Baba used to collect bhiksha and serve it to the devotees and eat himself too. He would grind wheat himself using this grinder, a practice in every house those days. Baba's photo, the original painting by Shyamrao Jayakar, is also installed here at the place where he used to sit. That big stone on which Baba used to sit is also seen in Dwarkamai, and a photo of Baba has been placed on it. There is a small tulsi-vrindavan (holy basil plant).

8. *Chavadi:* This is adjacent to the temple and was used as an alternate accommodation by Baba. On alternate days, he used to sleep in Chavadi and Dwarkamai. Otherwise it was used as a bhakta niwas. Now Baba's photo is installed there. Every day Baba used to clean both these places with a broom in his hand. He taught us about the cleanliness of the premises and town.
9. *Hanuman Mandir:* A big Dakshin Mukhi Hanuman Mandir exists adjacent to the temple premises. This has been there since Baba's time.
10. *Ganesh, Shani, Mahadev Mandir:* Inside the temple premises there are three small temples. In front of the Mahadev Mandir you will find a small statue of a tiger. It is in the memory of a tiger that was

brought to Baba. It was tied up strongly in chains. Baba asked that it be freed of chains. When that was done, the tiger climbed a few steps of Dwarkamai and died there. It was buried there, and thereafter the statue was installed in its memory in 1969. It is known as the Samadhi of a Tiger[34].

11. *Datta Mandir:* Sai Baba, Gajanan Maharaj of Shegaon, Swami Samarth of Akkalkot are all considered as part of the sect of Bhagwan Datta. Therefore there is a Datta Mandir inside the temple premises.
12. *Lamp Posts:* There are two such lamp posts in traditional style, where devotees place the oil lamps and ignite them. These are specially decorated on festival days, especially Diwali.
13. *Lendi Baug:* Baba was fond of planting trees and nurturing them. He had planted most of the trees in Lendi Baug. Some of them exist even today. He taught us the importance of environmental care and tree plantation.
14. *Shatabdi Dhwaj Stambh:* The flag post installed specially to hoist the Samadhi Shatabdi flag at the hands of the Hon. President of India has been installed in Lendi Baug. It has a base of 7x7 feet and is 150 feet tall. It has a background of an artificial waterfall. It is made of brass and is a point of attraction. The flag continues to be hoisted and is replaced twice a year.
15. *Bookstore:* There is a large bookstore inside the temple premises. All the publications of the Sansthan are available for sale here. *Shri Sai Satcharitra* authored by Govind Raghunath Dabholkar is available in

16 Indian languages and also in English. Books of aarti, bhajan and other stationery like calendars, diaries are available here.

16. *Parayan Hall: Shri Sai Satcharitra* is a sacred biography of Shri Sai Baba. It is close to the heart of the devotees. Many of them read it regularly. Reading it continuously is known as parayan. Total silence is maintained in this hall. Many devotees make it a point to go to the Parayan Hall, sit quietly and read some part of the *Sai Satcharitra*. Reading in the temple premises gives them immense satisfaction.
17. *Abhishek Hall:* Many devotees like to perform abhishek (holy bath to Sai Baba) at Shirdi. There is a facility to perform the abhishek pooja in the temple premises, which is a guided pooja coordinated by the poojaris of the temple. One has to take prior booking for this and perform it on the decided day.
18. *Shri Sai Satyavrat Pooja Hall:* Many devotees perform Shri Sai Satyavrat Pooja every day in this hall. It has to be pre-booked as it is very much in demand. To get the desired time slot on a specific day, one has to make a booking well in advance.
19. *Museum:* In my opinion, this is a place you must visit when you are in the Sai Baba Temple premises. It is located in Dixit Wada. Kakasaheb Dixit built this wada for the visiting devotees to stay. It was later converted into a museum. It has a ground floor and first floor heritage structure and now contains all the belongings used by Baba. Almost all the displays are more than a hundred years old. It has Baba's kafni

(shirt), paduka, chillum, palakhi, utensils, original photos of Baba and his contemporaries, etc.

20. *Meditation Centre:* This is a newly created facility. For a long time, it was on the wish list of the devotees. It is a cool, serene, silent and fully air-conditioned space. It can accommodate 200 devotees at a time. People go to this centre, sit quietly and try to meditate.
21. *Nanda Deep:* This is a lamp that has been burning continuously since Baba's time, in Lendi Baug.
22. *Blood Donation Centre:* We have talked about the blood donation scheme in an earlier chapter. The blood collection centre is located inside the temple premises. Four people can donate blood at a time. It is unique and a new pilgrimage for social scientists.
23. *Donation Counters:* Many devotees like to donate for the welfare schemes of the temples. There is a donation counter where you can donate in cash, cheque, DD, credit/debit cards, RGTS, online and so on. You instantly get a receipt of your payment.
24. *Donation Counting Hall:* This is yet another unique facility in the temple premises. The donations received by the temple in cash or kind are deposited in the hundis or donation boxes. There are 47 such donation boxes in the temple. The donation-counting methodology is highly transparent. Devotees, villagers, employees and banks participate in this process. There is a large hall in the basement of the temple. All the donation boxes are opened on the ground floor in the presence of witnesses and are emptied into a tunnel leading to the counting hall in the basement. There are appointed representatives

and bank employees in this hall, who then segregate the items into notes, coins, metal and coins of different countries. All the people in this hall wear a special uniform of a half-shirt and pyjama. The uniform is designed in such a manner that it has no pockets, no collar and no place to hide anything. They are checked by security at entry and exit and they cannot leave the hall until the entire process is completed. After counting, the money is handed over to the bank present on that day. The bank then issues receipts, collects the money and leaves. There are 15 banks involved in this process, and they are given the work by turns. The counting takes place twice a week on Tuesdays and Fridays. The amount so received is around ₹2–3 crores in every counting and is displayed at the donation counter. This place is not open for visitors.

25. *Strong Room:* This is used to store the gold and silver ornaments offered by devotees in a safe and secure manner. Multiple doors, entry–exit registers, operational records, CCTV surveillance, an alarm system and manual security are some of the features of the strong room. It holds around 500 kg gold and around 5,000 kg silver.
26. *Udi:* This is the sacred ash generated in the continuously burning dhuni (fire). This dhuni, as mentioned above, was ignited by Baba Himself, and it has been burning continuously since. Mostly cow dung is used as fuel in the dhuni. The ash is sieved, and only fine ash is used as udi. The udi so generated is packed in a small sachet with the help of machines. Udi is very much in demand.

Devotees take it home as Baba's prasad. It so happened that it was in short supply. Only about 50,000 sachets could be produced in a day, and the same would be distributed, so there would be no stock. When I visited this small plant, I noticed that each sachet contained 1.5 g of udi. I decided to reduce the quantity to 1.0 g. The result was that the daily production of sachet increased to 75,000 immediately and the situation was eased.

27. *Horse:* There is a statue of a horse called Shyamsunder in Lendi Baug. This horse used to participate in the Palkhi Yatra every Thursday.
28. *Gates:* The Mandir premises have five large gates numbered one to five. Gates 1 and 5 are for VIP movements and 2 and 3 are for devotee movements. Gate 4 is reserved as an additional gate and is opened occasionally.
29. *Aarti, ISO, Pooja-Vidhi:* The Temple has a disciplined schedule that everyone has to follow. Four aartis are performed every day. They are called Kakad Aarti (at 4:30 am), Madhyanya Aarti (at 12:00 noon), Dhoop Aarti (at sunset) and Shej Aarti (at 10:30 pm). The temple opens at 4:00 am and closes at 11:00 pm. All aarti, pooja, vidhi and other processes are standardised and documented in the form of ISO. The aartis, their sequence, beginning and end has been finalised and documented. All aartis are sung in chorus with the artists. Prior to Kakad Aarti, a recorded Bhupali is played (at 4:15 am). The temple is open for devotees from 4:00 am. Most of the rituals observed in the temple are of Vedic nature.

30. *Mangal Snan:* Just after the Kakad Aarti is over, Baba and the samadhi are given a bath every day (at 5:00 am) with warm water while singing Vedic mantras in Sanskrit. New clothes are draped, the Chhoti Aarti, 'Shirdi maze Pandharpur. . .' is sung, and then darshan begins.
31. *Palkhi:* Every Thursday, there is Palkhi Yatra at around 9:00 pm from the Samadhi Mandir to Dwarkamai/Chavadi and back.

Besides these, the security, CCTV control room, audio-visual broadcasting rooms and administrative offices are located inside the temple premises. This detailed information about the temple has not yet been documented in any book. So, the next time when you go to Shirdi, try to visit all these places.

4. SAI ANUBHUTI

19

Sai Controversy

Don't try to find the origin of a river or a saint

Recently, Shirdi and the Pathri village in Parbhani district of Maharashtra were at loggerheads over the controversy related to the birthplace of Sai Baba. Unfortunately, the Government of Maharashtra was drawn into this controversy because it announced a grant of ₹100 crores (₹1.00 billion) for the development of Pathri as the birthplace of Sai Baba. Finally, the government successfully pulled itself out of the controversy. This has created confusion among the devotees of Sai Baba, and they would definitely like to know the truth. So, I have tried to collect facts and present different viewpoints here.

Controversy is not new, neither to Sai baba nor to Shirdi. Sometimes somebody raises his voice and says something about Sai Baba. Just because the statement is about Sai Baba, the media will pick it up as news. Often these are mere publicity stunts. But recently, the residents of Shirdi and those of the village Pathri in the Parbhani district of Maharashtra raised the controversy about the birthplace of Sai Baba, and it continued for some time. Unfortunately, the Government of Maharashtra was drawn into this controversy because it announced a grant of ₹100 crores (₹1 billion) for the development of Pathri as the birthplace of Sai Baba. Finally, the government successfully pulled itself out of the controversy. This has created confusion among the devotees of Sai Baba, and they would definitely like to know the truth. So, I have tried to collect the facts and present different viewpoints here.

Second, it should be kept in mind that Shirdi is now a big commercial hub in the region. It has thousands of hotels, restaurants and banquet halls. It is also chosen for destination weddings. Almost every villager is a businessman. When I was moving around the temple premises some time back, I just enquired with a shopkeeper about the rent he pays to the owner. He replied, ₹10,000/-. I said that it was a good rent amount per month. His next statement opened my eyes. He said, 'Sir, it is not per month, we pay ₹10,000/- per day.' Many shops in this area are auctioned every day in the morning, and the shop is handed over to the highest bidder for doing business for that day. Often, the owner and the operator are different, even for hotels and restaurants. There is a continuous fear that Shirdi may lose its commercial importance. But I believe that no matter how many cities around Shirdi get developed, Shirdi itself will never lose its charisma since it is the karma bhumi of Sai Baba.

Now let us take a close look at the controversy about the birthplace of Sai Baba. There are two parties to the controversy. One is Pathri and the other is Shirdi. Proponents of Pathri have put forth some historical findings, authoritative statements and documented facts as follows.

The evidence put forth by Pathri contains 29 documents. (1) B.V. Narasimha Swamy's *Devotees Experiences of Sai Baba, Part 1*, All India Sai Samaj Madras, 3rd edition, 1965, has mentioned that Pathri as the birthplace of Sai Baba. (2) M.K. Gandhi in *In Search of the Supreme, Part 1*, Navajivan Publishing House, Ahmedabad, 1961, has also mentioned the same. (3) Eric H. Ericson's *Gandhi's Truth*, W.W. Norton and Co., 1969, has also mentioned the same. (4) B.V. Narsimha Swamy's *Devotees Experiences of Sai Baba*, part-3, page 9, mentions similarly that Sai Baba's birth place is Pathri. (5) G.R. Dabholkar's *Shri Sai Satcharitra*, Shri Sai Baba Sansthan, Shirdi, 8th edition, 1972, Chapter 7 page 13, mentions the same. (6) Swami Sai Sharanananda's *Shri Sai Baba in Gujarati*, 6th edition, 1966, Sterling Publication, New Delhi mentions the same. (7) B.V. Narsimha Swamy's *Tatraiva*, Part 2, page 46 mentions it. (8) Hari Sitaram Dixit's *Tatraiva*, page 1, mentions it. (9) *Shri Sai Leela*, in an article in April 1925, page 179, mentions it. (10) B.V. Narsimha Swamy's *Life of Sai Baba, Part 1*, 1955, mentions it. (11) *Shri Sai Leela*, September 1975, mentions it. (12) *Shri Sai Leela*, July–September 1942, pages 359–372, mentions it. (13) S.B. Dixit's *History of Indian Cosmology*, 2nd edition, 1931, mentions it. (14) Lt Col. Sir Wulses Heg's *The History of the Nizamshahi—Kings of Ahmednagar*, British Press India, Mumbai, 1923, mentions it. (15) Prof H.K. Sherwani and Dr V.M. Joshi's *History of Medieval Deccan, 1295 to 1724, Part-1*, Government of Andhra Pradesh, 1975, mentions it (16)

Lt Col. John Brig's *History of the Rise of Mohammedan Power in India Till A.D. 1612, Part 3,* mentions it. (17) M.V. Pradhan's *Shri Sai Baba of Shirdi*, Shri Sai Baba Sansthan, 7th edition, 1973 mentions it. (18) Vishwas Kher, a researcher, stated that Sai Baba's original name was Haribhau Parshuram Bhusari and he was born in 1938 in a Brahman family of Pathri. (19) Satya Sai Baba mentioned it in one of his speech in 1990. There are 10 other such documents[31].

The counter arguments are thus. (1) All the above documents are not research documents. No one has put forth any concrete evidence. Just a mention by anybody, be it B.V. Narsimha Swami or anybody else, cannot be taken as evidence. Most of the arguments are false or they are based on only logic and not the truth. It is just hearsay. (2) Vishwas Kher (son of the first CM of Maharashtra Balasaheb Kher), who has researched the subject and founded the Sai Janmasthan Trust in Pathri, has not put any truth before the public. His own statement in his document that 'This could be a possibility' itself indicates that he is not convinced, argues Mr Pramod Aher, who is the author of *Shirdi Gazetteer—The Untold Stories*[34]. (3) Sai Baba was in Shirdi for almost 80 years till 1918. No one had come forward during this period to state the name, birth date or birthplace of Sai Baba. (4) The only authorised document about Shri Sai Baba is *Shri Sai Satcharitra* written by G.R. Dabholkar. Sai Baba got it written by Dabholkar and approved it. It has no mention of his birthplace or name, etc. (5) The 8th edition of *Shri Sai Satcharitra*, which claimed to have the mention of Pathri as His birthplace, was somehow conspicuously missing from the Sai Baba Sansthan. Recently a copy of this edition was located with some employee, who presented it to Sansthan. But contrary to the statement, it does not have any mention of the birthplace of Sai baba. The original handwritten copy of the *Shri Sai Satcharitra* was handed over to the Sansthan recently by the heirs of G.R. Dabholkar, and the same was not found to have any mention of the birthplace of Sai Baba. (6) In one of the criminal cases in the Magistrate Court at Dhule, Sai Baba was called as witness, where he stated that his religion is Kabir and caste as Parvardigar, meaning God and did not talk about his name, birth place or family. (7) Ganesh Sahasrabuddhe, alias Dasganu Maharaj, has written in the biography of Keshavraj Babasaheb Maharaj about the birth of Sai Baba, but that again cannot be considered as evidence. (8) The *Sai Leela* is not a history magazine or a research journal. Nor are the writers research experts. A mere mention of something in the *Sai Leela* magazine does not make it authentic proof. There is no concrete evidence worth mentioning or considering seriously[32,33].

There are some more claimants who claim that Sai Baba's birthplace is Shri Vaikuntam in Tamil Nadu, Jerusalem-Jafa Darwaja in Gujarat and Pathri village in Andhra Pradesh, but all of them are without any basis. Some also say that Sai Baba was none other than Nanasaheb Peshve, who was missing since 1857 and was hiding from the British. All these claims will only entertain readers and nothing else.

The residents of Shirdi argue that they are not opposing the government grant or the development of

Pathri, but that their opposition is only to calling it the birthplace of Sai Baba.

Therefore, one has to categorically conclude that there is no proof for either the birth date, the birthplace or name, etc. of Sai Baba. The only authentic document on Sai Baba is the *Shri Sai Satcharitra* authored by G.R. Dabholkar, which does not contain anything on his birthplace, contrary to argument.

Our tradition specifically says that one should not try to find the origin of a river or a saint. Let us take some lessons from our traditional wisdom.

20

Sai Murti

Marble from Carrara village of Italy came for Baba's idol

It so happened that in 1952, a large, bright white block of marble was transported by ship from Italy to Mumbai Dockyard. It was not known who ordered it, and it lay unclaimed in the dockyard for a long time. Finally, the dockyard authorities decided to auction it. It was purchased by somebody and was donated to the Sansthan. The idea of making Baba's idol in marble was being discussed in Shirdi at the time. It was found that the marble block in Mumbai Dockyard was suitable for Baba's idol. It weighed around 6,000 kg. Quotations were invited from various artists capable of making idols. Finally, the work was assigned to Mr Balaji Vasant Talim.

You may like to know when and how the idol of Baba was installed in the Samadhi Mandir. It is an interesting story.

After Baba's samadhi, His photograph was placed in the Samadhi Mandir for devotees to take darshan and offer their prayers. The first management committee of the Sansthan was formed in 1925 under the leadership of Saint Dasganu Maharaj as the chairman. It was registered as a trust in 1934. Dasganu Maharaj continued to be the chairman till 1944. The committee was thinking of having Baba's idol made and installed in the Samadhi Mandir. Naturally, the construction material of the idol was the first thing to be discussed and decided. It was deliberated and decided that the idol should be made of marble. Long-lasting and good-quality marble was available only in Italy, known as Carrara marble. The Carrara village in Italy is famous for this marble and has a large number of hills with marble reserves. This is like the Makrana marble in Rajasthan which is abundantly available in the village Makrana of Rajasthan, India. How to get Carrara marble was a big question.

It so happened that in 1952, a large, bright white block of marble was transported by ship from Italy to Mumbai Dockyard. It was not known who ordered it, and lay unclaimed in the dockyard for a long time. Finally, the dockyard authorities decided to auction it. It was purchased by somebody and was donated to the Sansthan. The idea of making Baba's idol in marble was being discussed at the time. It was found that the marble block in Mumbai Dockyard was suitable for Baba's idol. It weighed around 6,000 kg. It is said that the block was transported from the dockyard to the studio by bullock cart, though it seems improbable. Quotations were invited from various artists capable of making idols. Talim, Wagh and Goregaonkar were the expert sculptors who presented their models made in clay. Finally, the model and the quotation of Mr Balaji Vasant Talim was selected and work was assigned to him[34].

The process of sculpting the idol started in Talim's workshop, called Talim Art Studio at Girgaon, near Opera House in Mumbai. The studio is on the ground floor and Mr Talim stays on the second floor of the same building. Sculpting the idol was not a simple task. Good-quality photographs of Baba were not available. Before making an actual idol in marble, the artist makes a model in clay. Then they make it in plaster of paris. Once the plaster model is finalised, a number of idols in marble can be made. The model was shown to the management committee, who liked it and asked him to proceed further.

The sculpting of the actual idol started with the involvement of a number of artists and specialists. Like doctors, there is a specialisation among sculptors too. One is a specialist in eyes, another in noses, faces, hands and so on. When the idol was ready, devotees began visiting the workshop. When nearing completion, it closely resembled Baba. Large numbers of devotees started pouring into the workshop and started offering flowers, etc. The studio was converted into a veritable temple. The idol is 5 feet tall and was installed on a platform which is 3.25 feet long and 2.5 feet wide. It cost ₹22,000/- (in those days) and the work took around seven months. Though the idol closely resembled Baba, the artist Balaji Talim was somehow not very happy and convinced because he thought that there was something lacking. One day, when he was sitting beside the idol deep in thought, he dreamed that Baba visited the workshop, sat beside His idol and granted darshan to him so that he could make an exact replica of Him. Now the sculptor was satisfied, and he gave the finishing touches to the idol and made it ready for delivery to the Sansthan.

The idol was transported to Shirdi on 2 October 1954, Saturday. From Khandoba Mandir, it was taken to the Samadhi Mandir in a grand procession. The idol installation was a grand ceremony that lasted for four days, from 5 to 8 October 1954. The installation ceremony was performed on 7 October 1954 at 7:30 am, which was Baba's Samadhi Day and also Dussehra, to the chanting of Vedic mantras[35].

The art of sculpting idols has been passed on for generations in the Talim family. Balaji Talim's son Mr Harish Balaji Talim, and now the grandson of Mr Rajiv Harish Talim, are also sculptors. They have preserved the plaster of paris model of Sai Baba in their workshop. The grandson has also sculpted a number of Baba's idols in marble for various Sai temples.

If the idol is to be protected from wear and tear, late Mr Sadashiv Gorakshar, a renowned curator who was director of the then Prince of Wales Museum (now known as Chatrapati Shivaji Maharaj Vastu Sangrahalaya) in Mumbai, suggested that the idol should not be exposed to the touch of hot and acidic fluids.

Devotees of Sai Baba often say that when you visit Sai temple in Shirdi and look at the idol of Sai Baba, you do not see just a marble statue. The idol appears to be alive and it starts talking to you!

21

Sai Anubhuti

Sai ways are not linear

Sai ways are unique. They are not linear, but criss-cross. In one of his 11 promises to His devotees, Baba said, 'Even though I am not physically present, I will take care of all my devotees.' This has resonated deeply with the devotees, and many devotees experience mystic happenings even today.

I have narrated a few experiences of devotees as they were communicated[36] by Dr Jitendra Shelke. These are their personal experiences and hence cannot be generalised. Each one will have different views regarding this. One must admit that each person has their own views, acceptances, shraddha. Let us respect them.

Baba has a Unique Connection with Everyone
(Dr Deepali Jaju; MBBS, MD, PhD

I live away from my motherland (India) in Muscat, Sultanate of Oman. In 2011, I met with a serious accident in Muscat. I was driving and another car hit my car from behind. My car was thrown to one side.

It hit a wall, toppled in the air thrice and then landed on the ground. While I was going through the accident, I saw that Baba was holding me in the air. I saw my body going through the accident. Once the car landed on the ground, Baba put me back in my body. This is my out-of-body experience. I didn't have a single scratch on my body. Once the car stopped, I opened the door and I came out. Baba changed my life.

I was alone at home. In 2015, I decided to do the parayan of *Sai Satcharitra*. I would get up at 4 am, complete the given parayan for the day and reach my hospital by 8 am. Two days went well. On the third day, I was too tired to get up. The alarm rang and I switched it off! Within the next few seconds, I got a strong kick in my back to wake me up! It was an unforgettable awakening. Who else could have given me the kick! I got up and completed the parayan.

I am from Shrirampur, a town near Shirdi. When I was a small child, there were no entertainment facilities or gardens in Shrirampur; so going to Shirdi on Sundays with parents was the best option. Shirdi was very different then, not so crowded as we see today. I refer to the years 1973–1980. I spent long hours, at times the whole day, in the big hall in front of Baba and would help pujaris in the temple as well. No one would object. I felt that I knew all the aartis. I have witnessed the foundation stone of the first hotel in Shirdi, but I cannot remember the name now.

For the last eight to nine years, I have started realising Baba's presence and how He gives awareness to one. There is a large gap between my childhood in Shirdi and my realisation of Sai. However, looking back, going through all the happenings of life, I feel, He was always there but I had no eyes and awareness to realise His presence. Sai has given me numerous experiences. Having trust in Him and being open and near to His consciousness is more important than being physically with Baba. Physical distance from Sai does not matter. Through every experience, Baba has taught me to distinguish between the mind, desires and the soul very clearly. When we are with our soul, clarity of thoughts, strength, patience, awareness, everything follows.

While working as a doctor, while teaching my medical and nursing students, or at home or with friends and society, Baba guides all throughout. When it comes to understanding the true reality or the consciousness, He helps me sail through perfectly. It is difficult to mention all the experiences here. Going through thousands of experiences with Baba, I feel Baba has a unique connection with everyone. We do not need any mediator to approach Baba. Call Baba with love and trust and He will be there for you. Accept what Baba gives you wholeheartedly.

It Was None Other than Shri Sai! (Shri Anant Sonthi, Boston, USA)

On 1 April 1992, I landed in Chicago, USA, with the aspiration of establishing a travel business in association with a friend. We started our office on 6 April 1992 in the Little India area of Chicago at Devon Avenue. With the divine blessings of Sai, my business is progressing well. In January 1993, I visited my home in Vijayawada. Along with my family and my friends' families, a total of 12 people—six adults and six children—visited Shirdi. My partner Pandu had booked the train tickets for all of us from Vijayawada to Manmad. From there we reached Shirdi at around 2 pm in the afternoon. Mr Pandu had booked our return journey for the same evening to Vijayawada. When we reached Shirdi, Sivaramakrishna from our group met his friend, who was returning from Shirdi. He told us that there was no aarti till the evening. So, returning to the train station the same day was not possible. I was not ready to return without attending Baba's aarti, so we cancelled the return tickets that we had booked. We then stayed at a hotel near the Maruthi Temple and attended the Shej Aarti (night aarti) that night. In the morning, we attended the Kakad Aarti and later the Madhyanya Aarti and then left Shirdi to reach the station for our journey home.

When we reached the station, we had no reservations for our return journey. The train was fully booked. We got general tickets and approached the TT. I contacted a railway officer and asked if he could help me get berths for our travel. When I told him that we were 12 people, including 6 children, he said the train was all booked and the chances were bleak. Then another railway officer who overheard my conversation with him said to me, 'If Baba wishes it, you will travel safely, don't worry'. We waited for the train to arrive. When it arrived, then the second officer approached me and asked all of us to board

Dining hall of the Prasadalaya at Shirdi

Solar-cooking system at Shirdi

Chapati-making machine

Design of Sai Baba Modern Educational Complex at Shirdi

Felicitating Hon. Suresh (Bhaiyyaji) Joshi, Sarkaryavah (All India General Secretary) of the RSS, along with Hon. Union Health Minister Harsh Vardhan

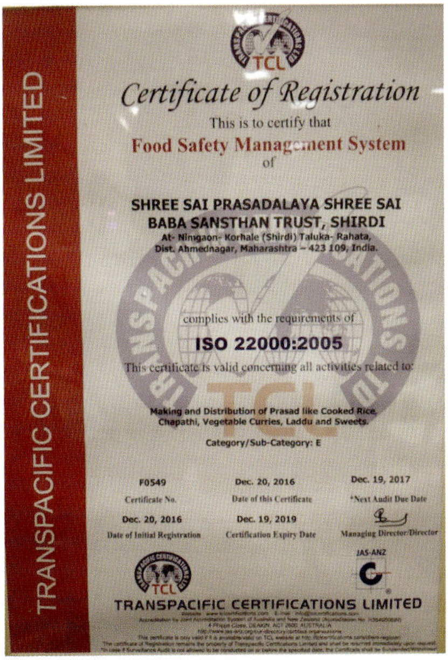

TRANSPACIFIC CERTIFICATIONS LIMITED

TCL

Certificate of Registration

This is to certify that

Food Safety Management System

of

SHREE SAI PRASADALAYA SHREE SAI BABA SANSTHAN TRUST, SHIRDI

At- Ningaon- Korhale (Shirdi) Taluka- Rahata, Dist. Ahmednagar, Maharashtra – 423 109, India.

complies with the requirements of

ISO 22000:2005

This certificate is valid concerning all activities related to:

Making and Distribution of Prasad like Cooked Rice, Chapathi, Vegetable Curries, Laddu and Sweets.

Category/Sub-Category: E

F0549	Dec. 20, 2016	Dec. 19, 2017
Certificate No.	Date of this Certificate	*Next Audit Due Date
Dec. 20, 2016	Dec. 19, 2019	
Date of Initial Registration	Certification Expiry Date	Managing Director/Director

JAS-ANZ

TRANSPACIFIC CERTIFICATIONS LIMITED

ISO certificate of the Prasadalaya

Felicitating Hon. Prakash Javadekar, Union Minister for Environment, Forest and Broadcasting

TRANSPACIFIC CERTIFICATIONS LIMITED

TCL

Certificate of Registration

This is to certify that

Quality Management System

of

SHRI SAIBABA SANSTHAN TRUST, SHIRDI (MANDIR)

At Post · Shirdi, Taluka Rahata,
Dist. Ahmednagar – 423 109, Maharasthra, India.

complies with the requirements of

ISO 9001:2015

This certificate is valid concerning all activities related to:

Provision of Puja Methods and other Rituals, Adherence to Tradition and Sanathana Dharma's, and Guiding the Devotees on Temple Seva Karyakrams, and providing Safety and Secure Environment to Devotees.

ANZSIC Code: 9540

13027	Mar. 06, 2017	Mar. 05, 2018
Certificate No.	Date of this Certificate	*Next Audit Due Date
Mar. 06, 2017	Mar. 05, 2020	
Date of Initial Registration	Certification Expiry Date	Managing Director/Director

TCL   IAF   JAS-ANZ

TRANSPACIFIC CERTIFICATIONS LIMITED

Website : www.tclcertifications.com E-mail : info@tclcertifications.com
Accreditation by Joint Accreditation System of Australia and New Zealand (Accreditation No. S2640303IN)
4 Phipps Close, DEAKIN, ACT 2600, AUSTRALIA
http://www.jas-anz.org/our-directory/certified-organisations
This certificate is only valid if it is available/valid on TCL website at http://tclcertifications.com/client-register/
The certificate of Registration remains the property of Transpacific Certifications Limited and shall be returned immediately upon request.
*In case if Surveillance/Recertification Audit is not allowed to be conducted on or before the specified date, the Certificate shall be Suspended/Withdrawn.

Version 1.11

ISO certificate of the Sai Samadhi Mandir

Students of Shri Sai Baba ITI at Shirdi

Inauguration of the Sai Agarbatti-making Project

Drying of flower petals in the green house for making agarbatti

Sai Sevak Scheme for devotee participation in Sai Seva

Proposed Sai Knowledge Park at Shirdi

A perspective of Sai Baba Samadhi Mandir, Shirdi

Inauguration of the Meditation Centre at Shirdi

प्रधान मंत्री

Prime Minister

MESSAGE

It is great to know that the centenary of the Mahasamadhi of Sai Baba is being observed at Shirdi under the auspices of Shri Saibaba Sansthan Trust.

The saintly life and teachings of Sai Baba continue to guide generations. His teachings encapsulate the spirit of harmony and his thoughts underline the spirit of oneness of humanity and universal love.

Best wishes for all the programmes associated with the Centenary celebrations.

(Narendra Modi)

New Delhi
06 October, 2017

Dr. Suresh Haware
Chairman
Shri Saibabasansthan Trust, Shirdi
Taluka- Rahata, District- Ahmednagar
Maharashtra- 423109

the ladies compartment. Till Daund station, that compartment was not full. Upon arrival at Daund station, he again came and ordered his associates to provide berths for us up to Secunderabad. We were given five berths and reached Secunderabad. In the afternoon, he again came to see us, wished us a safe journey to Vijayawada, and bid us goodbye. I believe, it is none other than Shri Sai who came in that form and took care of us on our journey back home.

When Sai Is There, Why Should We Fear
(Meenakshi Bhardwaj, New Delhi)

I want to share a personal experience of Sai. My younger son was seeking admission to an engineering (automobile) course at a good engineering college in Delhi. This was a great experience for me, especially because it was close to impossible for my son to get the admission as he had failed in Class XI examination due to some unavoidable circumstances. Those days were really difficult for me as a concerned mother. I was very worried for his future. And my son was adamant because all the circumstances held him responsible solely for his failure. As usual, my only resort was Sai.

I was very tense and spent sleepless nights worrying about his future; but holding my faith in Sai intact, confident that he would help me tackle this situation and that was why he had put me in this testing situation.

Sai answered me, as my son cleared the Delhi State Examination for admission to the engineering diploma course with a very good ranking on the basis of his Class X CBSE marks. Now he is about to complete his first-year course. He always wanted to do automobile engineering after school, but due to dirty politics by his class teacher, he was broken to the extent that he had lost interest in further studies.

When all his friends were applying for a good seat in colleges, Baba made me apply to this course. At the same time, I was able to convince my son to appear for this exam. This itself was a miracle, as he was not studying at all and he took the exam without any preparation. I kept reading Stavan Manjari at a mandir near his exam centre while I waited for him.

Another thing I want to share is that the result was declared on a Thursday, only confirming Baba's influence in all this. My son excelled. His admission day/induction day also fell on a Thursday. After admission, we visited the mandir which is just opposite his college.

What I found was Baba sitting on His throne with a broad smile asking me, 'Have you found all the answers now?'

I was visiting that mandir for the first time and was totally unaware that I would meet Baba in this mandir, which itself was another miracle for me. This indeed is a great miracle for me, as without wasting a year my son got admitted to an engineering college, where he would get direct admission to B.Tech. after completing the three-year diploma course.

All my son's friends were struggling for admission to good colleges and were able to get seats only outside Delhi while my son got a seat in a good engineering college without putting in much effort.

It is true that when Sai is there, why should we fear. Baba has proved that He will go to any extent to fulfil the genuine wishes of his devotees. When the world turned topsy-turvy for me and my son, my Sai stood by me and made sure that no harm was caused to me and my son. All hail to my Sai. Thanks for all the Grace mere Sai, all words fail to describe His Leela. Jai Jai ho Sai.

22

Superstition

Imagination is helpful

Imagination is an integral part of science. Now let us pose the question, what is zero? Obviously, it is nothing. Zero has no real existence. It is imaginary. But without zero, all of mathematics and science is zero. Though zero is imaginary, it is a useful tool to resolve many mysteries. The concept of zero was developed in India. Today, zero—both as a symbol or a numeral and a concept meaning the absence of any quantity—allows us to perform calculus and complicated equations and has helped us invent computers.

Somewhat misleadingly, superstitions are talked about with reference to Sai Baba. Some time ago, the news spread that an image of Sai Baba appeared on the wall of Dwarakamai in Shirdi Temple, where Baba used to stand. The security guard was the first to notice it. The news spread like wildfire and thousands of people gathered. Media persons would not miss such an occurrence. They too appeared to shoot the images. Many people saw something on the wall that resembled Sai Baba. The next day, the TV news channels were discussing this incident and they approached me for my opinion. I presented my views very logically. Here is an excerpt.

TV news channels were telecasting images shot in Shirdi. Perhaps the devotees imagined the resemblance between the image and Sai Baba. The news took it up as a human-interest story and even arranged talks and debates on this topic. There is a difference between perception and reality. Your perception may be real or unreal—there is a thin line dividing the two. Equally vague is the distinction between shraddha (faith) and andha shraddha (blind faith). Someone was once asked, what is the difference between a major operation and a minor operation. He replied in a light vein: if I am operated, it is a major operation, and if you are operated, it is a minor operation. Similarly, it can be said that my belief is shraddha and your belief is andha shraddha. This is how most people think.

Imagination is an integral part of science. Now let us pose a question, what is zero? Obviously, it is nothing. Can you give me zero rupees? You cannot. Zero has no real existence. It is imaginary. But without zero, all of mathematics and science is zero. Though zero is imaginary, it is a useful tool to solve many mysteries. The concept of zero was developed in India. Today, zero—both as a symbol or a numeral and a concept meaning the absence of any quantity—allows us to perform calculus and solve complicated equations and have helped in the invention of computers[37]. Therefore, imagination plays an important role in science as well. Similarly, one can ask, what is infinity? Infinity is an important concept in science, yet it is imaginary.

I recall the story of the benzene ring. There was a scientist called Kekule who discovered the structure of the benzene ring. One night, he dreamed that a snake was trying to catch its own tail in its mouth, but it kept failing. The snake tried many times but failed. He got up from a deep sleep and shouted 'Got it, got it!' He went to the office and designed the structure of the benzene ring, which is also incomplete. It was his imagination that helped him arrive at the structure of the benzene ring. The whole of organic chemistry is based on the structure of this benzene ring. Therefore, it is clear that imagination plays an important role in science.

There are superstitions in science too. Let us ask, what is dark matter? What is dark energy? Science does not know. Matter consists of particles. There are only three particles known to science, which are the proton, the neutron and the electron. The particulate nature of dark matter is not known to science[38]. The whole universe is made up of matter, and 85 per cent of it is dark matter. The universe has around 68 per cent of dark energy. How are the solar system and the galaxies created? Science posits the Big Bang Theory. Science demands repeatability and reproducibility. Can the creation of the universe be reproduced? Certainly not. Science still doesn't know with certainty what is at the bottom of the black hole[39].

Now let us take a simple day-to-day example. What is a virus? Medical science is silent about it. Doctors only say it may be a viral fever. And there is no treatment in medical science for the viral fever. Doctors only give symptomatic treatment. That means that if you have fever, you will be treated for fever but not for the virus.

If you have a cold, you will be treated for cold but not for the virus, and so on. And this is because medical science does not know what the treatment for a virus is. But it assumes something about it. So, science also operates on shraddha to a certain extent.

Incidents similar to the image on the wall have been reported: sometimes that Sai Baba's image appeared during the full moon and sometimes on the wall of a devotee's house in Canada. In my opinion, even the imagination or shraddha of Sai devotees should be respected. No one should disrespect anybody's shraddha. Each one has the right to have their shraddha. I have already explained that there is a thin line dividing shraddha and andha shraddha. There should be no place for andha shraddha. Let us learn to respect shraddha of each other. That is the only essence of this phenomenon.

23

Temple Management

> MBAs in temple management will make a difference
>
> *Just as marketing management, finance management and human resource management are taught in universities, temple management should also be taught. With this, we can create qualified human resources for management of temples. If MBAs and diploma or certificate holders in temple management are employed at the temples, they can inculcate discipline and organisation in the temple systems. It may also be noted that temples possess a huge potential for employment generation that has not yet been tapped. Training courses in temple management will make it possible.*

There are around 6.5 lakh (0.65 million) villages in India. While the number of schools and colleges in India is around 20 lakhs (2.0 million), the number of temples in the country is around 30 lakhs (3.0 million). These are only the major temples. If you include the small and roadside temples, the number may be in crores. It is interesting to observe that the number of temples surpasses the number of schools and colleges. It also gives us an idea about the scale of social influence temples can exert.

In the olden days, the temple used to be the centre of the town. If you go to Madurai and take a look at the Meenakshi Temple, you will get the idea. All the activities of the town would function around the temple. They had good reserves of water, which became the main source of water for the town. All personal and family ceremonies would be performed in the temple. In a way, temple would fulfil all the social needs of the individual. Today, these temples in India, taken together, generate huge wealth.

An observation of various temples reveals two common shortcomings. Naturally, there are exceptions, but these two shortcomings are generally apparent in most temples. The first is that these temples are unorganised, and the second is that they are undisciplined. Therefore, I perceive a need for formally teaching temple management. It should be taught at universities, just like courses in marketing management and finance management. Formal training will generate qualified human resources to manage these temples. MBAs and diploma or certificate holders in temple management can introduce discipline and organisation in the temple systems. Temples possess a huge potential for employment generation that has not yet been tapped.

Leaving out the exceptions, two major shortcomings can be identified when we visit temples. First, they are unorganised, and second, they are undisciplined. Therefore, I believe that the subject needs to be institutionalised. One of the many ways to do this is to include temple management in the universities. If trained individuals are employed, they can introduce discipline and organisation in the temples.

I have discussed this subject with the vice chancellors of some universities in Maharashtra. They liked the idea so much that if a course design could be created, they would implement it with immediate effect. When I started thinking about the curriculum, I realised the number of professions that a temple needs. There is a need of singers, pooja performers, poets to generate new aarti-pothi (literature), musicians, etc. Comparatively large temples also need finance managers, HR managers, material managers and so on. Take for instance the Balaji temple at Tirupati, which is the largest temple in India, where the annual turnover is more than ₹3,000 crores (₹30 billion). The temple has a total asset of around ₹90,000 crores (₹900 billion)[40]. It has more than 10,000 employees, the infrastructure is huge and the entire Tirumala Hills are owned by the temple. Their dharamshalas can accommodate around 40,000 devotees at a time. They require hundreds of barbers for head tonsuring as hair donation is considered a religious offering. When I enquired about what they do with the hair, I discovered astonishing facts. Hair is used to produce the vitamin keratin. It is also used in the film industry for wigs. The temple authorities auction the hair and earn more than ₹200 crores (₹2.00 billion) every year.

Now let us consider Shri Sai Baba temple in Shirdi, which is the second largest temple in India. Its annual turnover is around ₹700 crores (₹7.0 billion). It has around 5,000 employees directly and provides employment to thousands indirectly. It has a mega kitchen that can feed around one lakh people every day. This temple town has around 3,000 big and small hotels and thousands of restaurants. The temple runs two large hospitals with around 575 beds. On similar lines, you can consider the Golden Temple at Amritsar, Vaishnodevi Temple at Jammu, Shri Padmanabhaswamy Temple at Thiruvananthapuram, the chain of Swaminarayan Akshardham temples, the chain of Hare Rama-Hare Krishna Temples, Jagannath Temple in Puri, Siddhivinayak Temple in Mumbai, Somnath Temple in Gujarat, Sabarimala Ayappa Temple in Kerala, Kashi Vishwanath Temple in Varanasi[40] and so on. A temple is no less than an industry. The amount of finance involved is huge and so is the employment potential. This phenomenon is unique to India. No other country in the world is so rich in the number of temples or religious places.

Nowadays, many temples are managed through IAS cadre officers. Balaji Temple at Tirupati (Andhra Pradesh), Shri Sai Baba Temple at Shirdi (Maharashtra), Kanak Durga Temple at Vijayawada (Telangana) are some of the examples that are managed through IAS cadre officers. These IAS officers are trained in administration. Professionalism can be brought in by MBAs in temple management. Hence it is important to have formal courses in temple management.

The scientific and professional management of temples has been neglected in India for centuries, but the subject is of crucial importance in the present time. The purpose of this writeup is only to attract the attention of the professionals towards this necessity. And if it cannot be done in India, then it cannot be done anywhere else in the world.

24

Looking Back

> Service to the poor is true worship.

We love to boast that I did this or I accomplished that. Little do we know the truth. It is He who acts and He who makes us act. We are mere instruments of the Almighty, and through us, He accomplishes various things. This has been my belief all along.

It is my earnest feeling that the opportunity that I got to serve Sai is the biggest divine blessing of my life. Thoughts of Sai Baba constantly occupied my mind and I strove to fulfil his teachings. By harnessing science and technology, I attempted to address the changing needs of the devotees who visit Shirdi. The true worship of Sai Baba is through the service of poor and suffering individuals and by ensuring the welfare of society at large. All our endeavours have been focused on fulfilling this aspect of Sai Baba's teachings. There was a time when I rarely visited Shirdi. Now, I seemed to have only one destination—Shirdi. Earlier, I never used to think about Sai Baba. But, during this period, I thought of nothing other than Sai Baba. I was always pulled towards Shirdi. This experience completely transformed my life.

The years passed so quickly. Some visions were fulfilled, others remained incomplete. Whatever was accomplished was due to the blessings of Sai Baba and what remained incomplete was due to my shortcomings.

There is no joy greater than the service of Sai Baba. It is not only I but all Sai devotees who will tell you this. I learned through my experiences that the devotion to Sai knows no boundaries. At Shirdi, you meet many people who have had wonderful experiences—both in real life and spiritual ones. You only have to start a conversation, and the other person shares their astounding story. You come to realise that the devotion to Sai is manifested mainly through these spiritual experiences.

I am a sensitive person by nature. I take utmost care to see that I do not offend anyone, even through my words, spoken or written. But I am only human. During this period, if I have knowingly or unknowingly offended anyone, I sincerely request them to forgive me.

Om Sai Ram!

ENDNOTES

1. Parthasarathy, Avula. *The Fall of the Human Intellect*. Mumbai: A. Parthasarathy, 2015.
2. Parthasarathy, Avula. *The Holocaust of Attachment*. Mumbai: A. Parthasarathy, 2014.
3. Parthasarathy, Avula. *Vedanta Treatise: The Eternities*. 17th ed. Mumbai: A. Parthasarathy, 2015.
4. Sonali. 'Bhakti Movement: Meaning, Features and Impact'. History Discussion - Discuss Anything About History. August 8, 2015. https://www.historydiscussion.net/history-of-india/bhakti-movement-meaning-features-and-impact/2734.
5. Parthasarathy, Avula. *Bhagavad Gita*. 3rd ed. Mumbai: A. Parthasarathy, 2017.
6. Ayyavu, A. S. Legacy of Wisdom, April 10, 2020. http://legacyofwisdom.blogspot.com/.
7. 'What Were the 5 Principles Bhakti Tradition?'. Brainly.in. Brainly, n.d. https://brainly.in/question/14706312.
8. Aiyangar, Sridhar. '"Navavidha Bhakti"—The 9 Forms of Devotion to Attain the Supreme Lord'. Divya Pracharam, August 7, 2014. https://divyapracharam.wordpress.com/2014/08/06/navavidha-bhakti-the-9-forms-of-devotion-to-attain-the-supreme-lord/.
9. Dabholkar, Hemadpant. *Sai Satcharitra*. Shirdi: Shri Saibaba Sansthan Trust, 1930.
10. 'Shraddha (Faith): The Foundation of Spiritual Progress'. *Akhand Jyoti* 1 (2007). literature.awgp.org.
11. Swami Satchidananda. 'It All Boils Down to This One Thing'. The Golden Present, April 6, 2020. https://thegoldenpresent.org/.
12. Personal Discussion with Adv Arun Tripathi, Navi Mumbai, 29 October 2020.

13. Mehta, Kriti. 'Shraddha, Saburi: The Teachings of Sai Baba That Put Guru on High Pedestal of Reverence'. Mind and Soul. *Times Now*, May 7, 2020. https://www.timesnownews.com/spiritual/article/shraddha-saburi-the-teachings-of-sai-baba-that-put-guru-on-high-pedestal-of-reverence/588141.
14. 'You Are in Sai World—You Are in Sai World'. Saburi, May 19, 2020. https://saisaburi.org/.
15. Singh, Col. Gurnam. 'Patience Is the Essence of Spirituality'. Speakingtree.in. Speaking Tree, August 10, 2012. https://www.speakingtree.in/blog/patience-is-the-essence-of-spirituality-93456.
16. Rufus, S. 'Practice Patience'. Spirituality & Health, 2014. https://spiritualityhealth.com/articles/2014/02/18/practice-patience.
17. 'Tree Facts'. Growing Air. Accessed December 21, 2020. https://growingair.nl/facts/.
18. Singh, Vijai. 'What Is the Meaning of Hindi Phrase "Sabka Maalik Ek"?' Quora, October 29, 2017. https://www.quora.com/What-is-the-meaning-of-Hindi-phrase-Sabka-Maalik-Ek.
19. Marulkar Shaunak. 'Sab ka Malik Ek'. June 2, 2017. https://medium.com/@flywithshaunak.
20. 'Advaita Vedanta'. Internet Encyclopedia of Philosophy. Accessed December 21, 2020. https://iep.utm.edu/adv-veda/.
21. Bajpai, Prakash. 'EKAM SAT VIPRA BAHUDA VADANTI'. Speakingtree.in. *Speaking Tree*, August 19, 2012. https://www.speakingtree.in/blog/ekam-sat-vipra-bahuda-vadanti.
22. Christensen, Thomas H. *Solid Waste Technology and Management*. Chichester, West Sussex: Wiley, 2011.
23. Saleem, Wajeeha, Ayesha Zulfiqar, Muneeba Tahir, Fatima Asif, and Ghazala Yaqub. 'Latest Technologies of Municipal Solid Waste Management in Developed and Developing Countries: A Review'. *International Journal of Advanced Science and Research* 1, no. 10 (October 2016): 22–29.
24. 'What Is Anaerobic Digestion?' *American Biogas Council*. Accessed December 21, 2020. https://americanbiogascouncil.org/resources/what-is-anaerobic-digestion/.

25. 'National Estimation of Blood Requirement in India'. National Aids Control Organisation (NACO). India, March 2018.
26. Sharma, Milan. 'Why India Is Facing a Huge Blood Crisis'. *India Today*. India Today, November 17, 2019. https://www.indiatoday.in/mail-today/story/why-india-is-facing-a-huge-blood-crisis-1619927-2019-11-18.
27. Sadasivan, Suryaprabha. 'India Needs to Move towards an Altruism Based Voluntary Blood Donation Culture—ET HealthWorld'. ETHealthworld.com. *Economic Times*, October 1, 2019. https://health.economictimes.indiatimes.com/news/industry/india-needs-to-move-towards-an-altruism-based-voluntary-blood-donation-culture/71394034.
28. Sarkar, Suman. 'Artificial Blood'. *Indian Journal of Critical Care Medicine* 12, no. 3 (2008): 140–44. https://doi.org/10.4103/0972-5229.43685.
29. Haware, Suresh. *Saiseva—A Divine Blessing*. Mumbai: NavChaitanya Publication, 2019.
30. Satpathy, Chandra Bhanu. *New Findings on Shirdi Sai Baba*. New Delhi: Sterling Publications, 2019.
31. *Pathri karanche 29 purave, Daily Divya Bhaskar*. Nashik edition, 19 Jan 2020.
32. *Shirdikar Mhantat, Daily Divya Bhaskar*. Nashik edition, 20 Jan 2020.
33. Private Communication, Pramod Aher, Shirdi, September 2020.
34. Aher, Pramod. *Shirdi Gazetteer—The Untold Stories*. Shirdi: Yugandhar Publication, 2017.
35. Nagarsekar, Suresh. *Shri Saincha Darbar*. 2nd ed. , Mumbai: S. Nagarsekar, 2018.
36. Private Communication, Dr Jeetendra Shelke, Shirdi, September 2020.
37. Szalay, Jessie. 'Who Invented Zero?' LiveScience. Purch, September 18, 2017. https://www.livescience.com/27853-who-invented-zero.html.
38. 'Dark Matter'. CERN Accelerating science. CERN. Accessed January 20, 2020. https://home.cern/science/physics/dark-matter.

39. Staff, ScienceAlert. 'What Are Black Holes?' ScienceAlert. Accessed December 21, 2020. https://www.sciencealert.com/black-holes.

40. Barnwal, Amrita. 'Richest Temples of India: List of 12 Wealthiest Temples in India'. EaseMyTrip, December 3, 2019. https://www.easemytrip.com/blog/richest-temples-in-india.

ABOUT THE AUTHOR

DR SURESH HAWARE is a motivational business leader known for his organisational and administrative skills. He earned his BTech in chemical engineering from Nagpur University, Maharashtra, and completed his postgraduate studies in nuclear engineering from Bhabha Atomic Research Centre. Later, he did an MA in history. Recently, he has completed a PhD in affordable nano housing at Mumbai University. He is a merit scholar from Nagpur University and the winner of a gold medal in engineering from Nagpur University.

He served as senior nuclear scientist in the Department of Atomic Energy for 27 years. He has authored 37 research papers in nuclear engineering that have been published in prominent international and national journals. He led a team of Indian nuclear scientists to International Atomic Energy Agency, Vienna. He has been actively engaged in business for the last 25 years. He presently owns and leads the reputed Haware Group of Companies. He has initiated several philanthropic activities.

Dr Haware has served as a trustee for Jawaharlal Nehru Port, India's largest port. For the last four years, he has been the chairman of Shri Sai Baba Sansthan Trust, Shirdi, Maharashtra, India's second-largest temple. He has won more than 29 prestigious international and national business awards and has authored 10 books on business/entrepreneurship. He has created, anchored and presented two TV serials on business, each with 20 episodes.

An avid mountaineer, Dr Haware has scaled Island Peak Mountain in Nepal up to 6,120 m. He has trekked up to Mount Everest Base Camp.